Sollars writes profoundly about leading toward and away from .... up with a great tradition of writing that affirms the depths of the human condition and attempts to delineate factors that enable sound development. The author contributes to a basic concern in literature and spirituality involving the corruption one undergoes in order to survive, while an unblemished element of selfhood remains.

Michael Eigen
Author of *Faith, The Psychotic Core, The Birth of Experience*

Franklin Sollars has written a profound, important book that offers insight into the possibilities of a unified spiritually oriented psychotherapy that addresses the essential Core Self of a human being, a Core Self that fulfills itself through unity. His model is alchemical transformation of the Core Self, and he draws inspiration from psychoanalysts such as Wilfred Bion, Michael Eigen, Gerald J. Gargiulo, and James Grotstein, and joins their ranks as a major contributor to writers who consider the relationship of the spiritual self and psychotherapy.

Merle Molofsky
Psychoanalyst, Faculty member of the Harlem Family Institute; Faculty member of the Training Institute NPAP, Board of Directors of the International Forum for Psychoanalytic Education, and the Advisory Board of Harlem Family Institute, author of *Streets 1970*.

Franklin Sollars's writing takes us beyond the important healing of early damages and resulting defenses. He shows us the exciting potential of our Core Self in unitive consciousness.

Eugene F. Humphrey, PhD
Senior Pathwork Helper

Love Outraged
and the
Liberation of the Core Self

*An integrative depth psychological approach for emotional
growth and spiritual development*

Franklin Sollars, PhD

University
PROFESSORS PRESS

Love Outraged and the Liberation of the Core Self
By Franklin Sollars

First published in 2016, University Professors Press

ISBN-13: 978-1-939686-12-1

University Professors Press
Colorado Springs, CO
http://www.universityprofessorspress.com

Cover Photo by Franklin Sollars
Cover Design by Laura Ross, 2016

Reprint Permissions:
Sollars, F. R. (2014). The core self in psychoanalytic literature and its benign and ideal dimensions. *International Journal of Behavioral Research & Psychology, 2(*4), 40–46. doi: 10.19070/2332-3000-140008. (Copyright Franklin R. Sollars)

Sollars, F. R. (2013). A further elaboration of needs in psychoanalysis: Needs in conflict, compromise, and harmony. *Psychoanalytic Review, 100,* 217–237. (Reprinted with permission from Guildford Press.)

Table of Contents

Foreword

In this beautifully crafted, meticulously researched study that interweaves two healing paths, spiritual development and compassionate psychotherapy, Dr. Franklin Sollars has written a new guide for the perplexed, a description of the fulfilling of human potential in the twenty-first century. He offers insight into the possibilities of a unified spiritually oriented psychotherapy that addresses the essential Core Self of a human being, a Core Self that fulfills itself through unity.

The concept of Core Self is both familiar and innovative. As we contemplate the term, something within our own core resonates with what we perceive and believe to be immutable, natural, and true, a necessary element of our being—thus, familiar. And yet old ways of thinking, easy platitudes, do not enliven the concept. Indeed, ready-made assumptions of what we mean by Core Self can shut down our imagination. Dr. Sollars offers an innovative way of discovering what we will awaken to when considering the Core Self. He easily draws on spiritual concepts and psychological concepts, and creates a definition both simple and complex. In his Glossary, he defines Core Self as "the expansive foundational self in all human beings that rests in unitive experience of love and primary connectedness with others."

His definition roots itself in quotidian possibility, a natural state of being, and as we contemplate his meaning and begin to read, we recognize that this aspect of our birthright is not always available to everyone, although it can be restored.

Dr. Sollars readily takes on the challenge of exploring the depth and beauty of spiritual insight, within a context of psychological understanding. In describing and elaborating on spiritual experience, he leads us on a journey across many cultures, many geographies, many centuries. He offers us great wisdom when he says that "What we are most deeply afraid of is not inadequacy or low self-worth; nor is what we are most deeply afraid of our wickedness or cruelty. What we are most deeply afraid of is our loving, powerful, creative self. That is our spiritual self, our core self" (p. 7). This statement has both shock value and reassurance. We read it, draw in our breath, and wonder, and we also recognize within this wisdom that we can endure the wonderful quality of our deepest fear. Dr. Sollars offers us access to something we want to know about ourselves.

In his discourse, Dr. Sollars offers us a steadily murmuring subtext meditation on unification. Discussing unity and duality, he draws on the riches of many spiritual traditions—Buddhism, Taoism, Sufism, Mystical Christianity, Kabala—and within these traditions he leads us to contemplate shame. In contemplating shame, he brings us into the profound psychological discoveries beginning with Sigmund Freud in the late nineteenth century and continuing into the twentieth century with the many elaborations of psychoanalytic thought. His model is alchemical transformation of the Core Self, and he draws inspiration from psychoanalysts such as Wilfred Bion, Michael Eigen, Gerald J. Gargiulo, and James Grotstein, and joins their ranks as a major contributor, taking his place as one of the gifted writers who consider the relationship of the spiritual self and psychotherapy.

This new guide for the perplexed reminds us that we have the potential to live in a unified state, which is characterized by a sense of peace, and that we can attain this, not as a steady state, because no state is a steady state, but as an accessible, meaningful liberating possibility that we attain by dedication to the search. We are offered a detailed description of spiritually oriented depth psychology, a healing path that will liberate a Core Self, releasing the Core Self to live within the possibility of unitive love. In considering the vicissitudes of love and libido discussed in psychoanalytic theory, Dr. Sollars reviews the earliest contributions, and later elaborations, of Sigmund Freud, and from there the contributions of many others, returning ultimately to the underlying notion of transformation, the matrix where spirituality and depth psychotherapy meet.

Dr. Sollars takes us to the transformational matrix with a model he recognizes as basic and simple, and which proves, ultimately, to be relevant and useful. Using a visual image of a cosmic egg, he examines the relationship among Core Self, Lower Self, Ego, and False Self. Each has a psychical function. His model covers major concepts found in spiritual systems and psychoanalysis in a glorious mix-and-match array. For instance, in this dance of ideas, he introduces the concept of soul as Plotinus describes it, the higher soul leading the lower soul out of the depths, the lower soul encompassing Freud's id and Jung's shadow, psychotic process as described by Michael Eigen, a delightful mingling of concepts from the riches of Western civilization.

The further we wander into the delightful complexities of this book, the more we encounter talismanic representations of the best of spiritual and psychological adventuring, with Dr. Sollars as Virgil to our Dantean Core Self, showing us the splendors and terrors of the mind. Along with Dr. Sollars and Wilfred Bion, we encounter the transformation of beta into alpha elements. At other points in the book, we encounter negativity. We encounter trauma and the vicissitudes of experience, with hate as well as love predominating at times. We encounter pathogenic belief systems. Dr. Sollars reminds us that "childhood hurts." And yet, as we stay on the path with him, our perplexity yields to a sense of unity in the manifestation of love. We may encounter what he calls the marriage of pleasure and pain, the enduring self-punishment of perpetual guilt. Nonetheless, using the wisdom of spiritually informed psychotherapy, Eros will predominate.

A favorite passage of mine in this book is an anecdote describing Dr. Sollars' grandson David, two years old at the time, encountering his beloved Aunt Dee Dee (p. 168). The discovery within the child of his mixed feelings of love and anger, the confusion that anger at a loved one can generate, Aunt Dee Dee's recognition of the child's complexity of feeling when guided by Dr. Sollars to do so, is poignant and enriching. We all can learn from this all too familiar scenario, when it is moderated by someone with the depth of understanding that permeates this book.

Merle Molofsky
New York, NY

Preface

Early in my own search for spiritual and emotional growth, after examination of various spiritual schools, it became apparent that while all were helpful each lacked enough power or the right kind of "medicine" to help me overcome personal hurdles. These hurdles included my own personal shadow and darkness that needed to be understood, contained and transformed. Simultaneously my studies in psychotherapy, which took me through Humanistic and Phenomenological schools and eventually psychoanalytic training, left a sort of hole or emptiness regarding my longing for spiritual understanding and growth. Consequently, I began a parallel track in my life's work of attempting to integrate spirituality and mysticism with a depth psychological approach to marrying these two important needs of mine. This book is an outpicturing of my study and experience in the most succinct and readable form that I could accomplish without losing too much depth and texture regarding these important subjects.

There are popular spiritual paths for those wanting spiritual growth that I believe promise a lot without expecting much of the seeker. I think they are helpful to a point. However, serious and earnest students who seek growth need more, and I have worked to provide some help toward this need. I have attempted to reach psychologically minded spiritual seekers within the text as well as speak to graduate students and psychotherapists who are seeking an integrated model of spirituality and depth psychology to help them with their work. Newer students or seekers may find some resonance with the first read but may circle back and find more depth of understanding as they study the text with some purpose. For those who have an understanding of spirituality and depth psychology I hope it immediately speaks to you and finds depth and resonance with your needs.

Within the text you will find a model of personality theory that is an integration of psychoanalytic and spiritual schools. You will find case examples of people struggling with deep shadow elements that are beyond help with simple positive visualizations, affirmations or mere cognitive work. Many of the people mentioned require a depth understanding of their unconscious to gain some measure of control and transformation of their shadow elements. In the section called Prometheus Bound, I discuss a depth approach to deal with people who are stuck in their search for spiritual and emotional health and can't seem to find a way forward. Some meditations are provided that will help with your own spiritual and self-analysis and can also be applied to psychotherapy. I also engaged in recorded dialogue with some very gifted people who asked pertinent questions about aspects of the approach I describe in this book that I believe many will find helpful. There are many other interesting elements I will leave you to discover.

Thanks for reading,
Franklin

Introduction

If you want to awaken all of humanity,
then awaken all of yourself.
If you want to eliminate suffering in the world,
* then eliminate all that is dark and negative in yourself.*
For truly, the greatest gift you have to offer humanity,
is your own transformation.

~Lao Tzu (1988)

This book is written to help all those seeking spiritual and psychological growth in various ways and feel they could use a more depth psychological approach to move them along on their path. It is written for deeply psychologically minded people—people who are in therapy, spiritual seekers, students studying psychology and psychotherapists alike. I have attempted to write the book, which although difficult at times, is readable for seekers, those who are on spiritual paths, and also those psychotherapists who might want a different lens with which to see their clients in order to help them with their growth. My intention for the book was not to develop a deep and profound philosophical or psychological treatise but to provide a gateway, perhaps a primer, for seekers, students and curious therapists to engage in a depth process of spiritual transformation. This depth psychological approach is provided as an alternative to approaches that seek a fast-food-like consumption of spiritual transformation that results in bypassing the depths of our being.

I suggest it is an integrative approach to spiritual /psychological growth because it draws from many spiritual circles such as Buddhism, Mystical Christianity, the Kabala, Sufism, to name a few, and on the psychological approaches of psychoanalysis, humanistic psychology, and transpersonal psychology. This is an interesting mixture, which many psychotherapists may find to be irreconcilable.

However, I take a syncretic approach, which embraces the idea that there is an underlying unity to be discovered in all these apparently contradictory approaches. I hope you will see this unity emerge as you read the text.

This is not a book that requires nothing of the reader or the practitioner of its approach. To use it most effectively, it requires at least a modicum of self-reflection and self-examination. It also requires what the Poet John Keats has called *negative capability*, which is the ability to remain with doubt and uncertainty when self-reflecting and not rush to easy ready-made answers. Perhaps even more than negative capability it requires negative containment. That is, the ability to recognize and to entertain unflattering thoughts, impulses, faults and insights, in the faith they can be understood and resolved without covering them over or rationalizing them. Enough discipline must emerge to do a little work on yourself, in the confrontation of your faults, and those personality elements that hold you back from your vibrant and loving core. No enduring emotional or spiritual growth can be accomplished with this or any approach without dedication, discipline and self-examination.

There are many paths to the top of the mountain; this, true seekers realize. For those who honestly seek, the path is steep and narrow and does not come easy at first but, with perseverance, liberation and joy are possible. This particular path has worked well for me, and I hope it will be of help to you. This is the spirit in which it is offered.

I would like to thank my many teachers over the years for help in the development of this book, including my clients and supervisees as teachers. I would also like to thank the historical teachers who labored in their times to bring us wisdom and inspiration that has helped us on our paths of spiritual and emotional growth. Thanks also to those of the spirit who helped in the development of the text and helped guide you along your journeys. May you all be blessed and inspired to continue on your paths and in the liberation of your core self.

Chapter 1
Introduction to the Core Self

True spirituality is not a high, not a rush, not an altered state. It has been fine to romance it for a while, but our times call for something far more real, grounded, and responsible; something radically alive and naturally integral; something that shakes us to our very core until we stop treating spiritual deepening as something to dabble in here and there. Authentic spirituality is not some little flicker or buzz of knowingness, not a psychedelic blast-through or a mellow hanging-out on some exalted plane of consciousness, not a bubble of immunity, but a vast fire of liberation, an exquisitely fitting crucible and sanctuary, providing both heat and light for the healing and awakening we need.

~ Robert Augustus Masters

Psycho-spiritual growth from the perspective I am advocating requires personality transformation. It requires the transformation of the negative traits and faults we find in ourselves to positive life-affirming virtues. Transcendence is often pursued, mostly by those who want spiritual growth to come easily, instead of transformation, by choosing the rather exclusive use of meditative practices or the ascetic avoidance of life's troubles over a depth psychological approach. The transcendent approach may be helpful for emotional growth and liberation, but it can also leave behind major elements of our personalities so that in times of stress and life's disturbances we fall prey again to our vanity, pride and fears. While many ardent spiritual seekers have noticed this leaving behind of undeveloped aspects of ourselves in the transformation process, many otherwise evolved teachers have come undone when some of the stressors and seductions of the material world impinged on their apparent equanimity. This phenomenon of leaving behind many undeveloped aspects of ourselves, which later come back to haunt us, has recently been identified and elaborated by the authors John Wellwood (1984) and Robert Augustus Masters (2010) as *spiritual bypassing*. One can be very advanced in spiritual growth in terms of developing a sense of peace, emotional balance and harmony when times are good, yet leave behind elements that catch us in the tempest of our worldly winds. In no way do I mean to disparage meditative techniques. I do, however, think more can be done in the way of bringing our overall personality along to catch up with the heights we may achieve in meditation. This is the path of transformation. Master's point of view so resoundingly rings in my ear:

> Any spiritual path, Eastern or Western, that does not deal in real depth with psychological issues, and deal with these in more than just spiritual contexts, is setting itself up for an abundance of spiritual bypassing. If there is not sufficient encouragement and support from spiritual teachers and teachings for practitioners to engage in significant depth in psychoemotional work, and if those students who really need such work don't then do it, they'll be left trying to work out their psychoemotional issues, traumatic and otherwise, only through the spiritual practices they have been given, as if doing so is somehow superior to—or a "higher" activity than—engaging in quality psychotherapy. Psychotherapy is often viewed as an inferior undertaking relative to spiritual practice, perhaps even something we shouldn't have to do. When our spiritual bypassing is more subtle, the idea of psychotherapy may be considered more acceptable, but we still shy away from a full-blooded investigation of our core wounds. (p.4)

Transformation is alchemical as the Thrice Great Hermes of the Middle Ages might suggest. Like the transformation of lead into gold, by way of the "philosopher's stone" of a depth psychological approach to spiritual development we can transform character faults, negativity and unhappiness into virtue, positivity and happiness in an enduring way. Rather than skipping over these character faults in wishful thinking that they really do not have to be dealt with, we practice spiritual transformation not simply by paying lip service to our desire for spiritual growth but by the work of self-examination, self-confrontation, embrace of negative capability and persistence in the pursuit of growth, come what may. This steep and narrow path is best suited to lift the shroud of negativity and fear that covers the divine spark in us—our core self.

There are spiritual paths, such as the *eightfold noble path* of Buddhism or the work of the Kabala, which I embrace and admire, but these and many other religious or spiritual paths lack the profound psychological insight and tools of twenty-first century depth psychology. Such tools can help immensely with our transformation. Without these tools, many a psycho-spiritual aspirant flies too close to the sun and, like Icarus, falls to the ground as his wings melt from the closeness to the divine. The proximity to peaceful, harmonious, divine existence becomes impossible to maintain when fears, resistances and demons, untransformed yet hidden, remain present.

Among the tools I am referring to are the understanding of psychological defenses, resistances, and unconscious motivation; elaborating and differentiating our emotions out of an undifferentiated mass of feelings; embracing the darkness in our self and articulating it; facing needs in conflict and compromise; discovering the process of mourning in emotional healing, and so forth. With our eyes on the prize of spiritual development, these powerful tools can be put in the service of transforming ourselves so that we emotionally embrace the unity of self and other, feel more at peace with ourselves, and gain a more powerful felt sense of the sacredness of life.

The Spiritual Path

Paradoxically, it is by recognizing ourselves as "utterly and merely human" that we open up to the divine within... This is why the path of spiritual evolution is really a path of self-discovery and self-purification. We find our own way, step by step, through our own personality towards ever greater spirituality.

~ *Eva Pierrakos*

What we are all most deeply afraid of is not inadequacy or low self-worth; nor is it our wickedness or cruelty. What we are most deeply afraid of is our loving, powerful, creative self—that is, our spiritual self, our core self. While fear of inadequacy and wickedness may haunt all of us in certain measure, it is a result of perhaps a more subtle yet deeper fear of surrendering to our love, our happiness, and our creative power, To those not psychologically minded, this may seem preposterous,. But when you have the ability to look deep into your psyche, you find that wickedness and even cruelty accrue from our *love outraged* by psychological injury—usually in our early psychological development. Even our inadequacy and low self-esteem accrue from ways in which we are frightened by love. When we are truly loving and connected deeply with our loving creative power we do not feel inadequate; we feel inspired and vital.

The fear of the most loving and best within us rests with our past psychological injuries and that we allow these injuries to keep us separated from these same loving impulses. Psychic injury causes pain, which leads to a numbing of our core of love. Psychological defenses, false pride, envy, indifference and even character faults defend against the awareness and containment of our pain and psychic injury—and the love outraged within them. Even cruelty is a way to dupe us into feeling that we don't care about others, when we always do. In addition to the release that the expression of cruelty gives us, it defends us from feeling real guilt about the separation from our loving feelings.

This spiritual/psychological approach leads us back to our core loving self, which lies embedded within our psychological distortions and defenses. The liberation process is an attempt, after we become acquainted with our shadow, to delicately remove the outer robes of defense that keep our light covered and sullied. The liberation process is intended to transform our negative defensive selves, after we have accepted them, back into love, light, and freedom. In Kabalistic and Gnostic lore, we are all considered divine sparks that, through life learning, need to be uncovered and connected back with the light.

When the depth project is viewed not just as a vehicle to cure neurosis or psychosis but as a way to embrace and contain the darkness within us so as to eventually transform it and liberate our inner light, it has become a spiritual path. When it is applied not just as a cure for depression or even simply unhappiness but primarily as a tool to liberate our joy and our creative vital self connecting us with the invigorating lifestream of emotions, intuition and vitality, it has become a spiritual path.

The spiritual path has always been with us, just as our inner seat of inspiration has always been. There is a relationship between this inner seat of inspiration and the spiritual path. The spiritual path has most often been about finding our way back to our spiritual self through self-examination and transformation, as opposed to many formal religious approaches that encourage worship and obedience and proclaimed faith. Those who practice worship, obedience, meditation and even prayer, which are all valuable, in isolation of self-transformation will still find it very difficult to attain the deep emotional growth that brings our feeling selves in line with our beliefs. It is easy to say "love your neighbor as yourself." It is much harder to actually feel it and live the experience in a deeply felt way.

Today, there are psychoanalysts and psychotherapists who seek a more spiritual basis for their life's work. There are also many psychologically minded lay people who seek psychotherapy, at least in part, for an answer to their spiritual journey. They often go looking for ways not only to cure psychological problems but also ways to make life more meaningful. Sometimes they have tried many other paths to the top of the mountain and have been left feeling lost and still looking for answers to their search. This book is an attempt to bridge the gap for these souls. It is an attempt to help spiritualize psychotherapy and provide a psychological basis and praxis for spiritual work out of the profoundly transformational experience of a depth psychological approach to psycho-spiritual growth.

In no way do I want to suggest that this is the only form a depth psychological approach to spiritual advancement can take. Any approach that addresses the lower unconscious element of the human personality and that simultaneously keeps its eye on the prize of spiritual advancement would be very helpful in bringing the entire personality along with spiritual growth. When lower elements are addressed, the chance of leaving behind character faults and egoism, which eventually bring down an otherwise advanced personality, are minimized. This is a coherent perspective based on a historical understanding of mystical approaches to spiritual growth and a more recent look at depth psychology. This framework has worked for me, and it is offered in whole or in part as a method that, I hope, will be helpful to a broad range of seekers and helpers.

A Brief Look at Depth Psychology

Eugene Bleuler is credited with the original framing of the term *depth psychology*. In 1910, in the Yearbook for Psychoanalytic and Psychopathological Investigations, under the title "Die Psychanalyse Freuds," Erik Craig credits him for mentioning depth psychology or its cognates at least 20 times (Craig 2008, p. 229). Depth psychology was quickly picked up by Freud, who later stated that Bleuler was speaking of nothing other than psychoanalysis when he coined the term, but others such as Adler (1927), Jung (1951, 1968), and Rank (1945, 1973) quickly evolved their own depth psychologies. Ego psychologists such as Heinz Hartmann (1954) and Karen Horney (1945, 1950), followed suit. Subsequently, with the advent of Object Relations theory, Melanie Klein (1975), Donald Winnicott (1965a, 1965b), Ronald Fairbairn (1994) and Michael Balint (1992) developed their own versions of depth psychology based on object seeking. Heinz Kohut (1971, 1977) also formulated a depth psychology based on a developmental theory of self-cohesion and parental/child interaction. Intersubjective/relational theory (Greenberg, 1991; S. A. Mitchell, 1988; Atwood & Stolorow, 1984; Stolorow & Atwood, 1992) grew out of a combination of interpersonal, object relational and self-psychological theory and focused on the primacy of the current relationship for therapeutic change. The intersubjective/relational approach echoes earlier existential humanistic approaches to depth psychology, including those of Ludwig Binswanger, (1963) Medard Boss (1963, 1979), R.D. Laing (1962, 1967), Rollo May (1969, 1975) and James Bugental (1965, 1976).

What all these forms of depth psychology have in common is a view of the human personality as complex and dynamic: complex in terms of multiple forms of motivation, including such impulsions as needs, drives, wants, wishes, desire, and affects; dynamic in that these impulses often contradict as well as complement one another, thus rendering the personality as conflicting and desiring in ways of which we are often unaware. These impulses we are often unaware of emanate from what is typically called the unconscious. This view of the person captures our multifaceted, ever complex, and mysterious personhood. Nothing less or more simplistic offers as much power to affect change that resonates from surface to depth in the personality and makes real transformation possible, and not just an ideal or a mask we want to present to ourselves and the world.

Regardless of how one practices, psychotherapy as a spiritual approach is profoundly limited as long as practitioners insist on locating a patient's difficulties exclusively within a one-person identified psyche without integrating the patient's relationship to a reality larger beyond the self. To that end, relational or intersubjective techniques fit well, as the metapsychology they are founded on is a belief in the mind as a two-person construct. Thus, you might say, these schools inherently embrace an expanded and more dual-track notion of self. These theories place the therapist–client relationship in the forefront of therapeutic change rather than on a totally intra-psychic approach of classical psychoanalysis. From this perspective the therapist's needs, foibles and strengths are taken into consideration along with the client's and are brought into the fray of reenactments of trouble spots within the relationship. This also closely resembles many existential humanistic approaches, which bring the needs and feelings of the therapist into play. Of course, this is not done as therapy for the therapist, but by registering the therapist's issues and reactions and even real feelings and needs as part of the therapeutic environment, it dispels the idea to a great degree that the therapist is the expert with a God's eye view of treatment and replaces it with two human beings in a relational dialogue meant to enrich the growth of the client.

Where I might differ philosophically with much of relational/ intersubjective psychotherapy is that I proffer a preexistent, unambivalent, unitive level to the self that lies waiting underneath our faults and defenses, and the belief that the core self is discovered, perhaps articulated, as much as constructed. The position that feelings, thoughts and wishes have a preexistent quality also ironically has an intersubjective element that seems to be unnoticed in much of the literature. That is, if we understand that we all share in these feelings that are present at some level of existence, much as a river we step into, it helps us leave our egocentricity behind. Instead of seeing ourselves as an isolated particle in a hostile or indifferent universe that has nothing to do with us, we can move to feeling the unity between others, the universe and ourselves. To know that we partake of feelings and beliefs that have been shared by humanity, not just currently but historically, can help us leave our narcissistic, isolating walls and facilitate an embrace of our common archetypal connection—the sense of union discussed in this manuscript.

In the liberation of the core self with its sense of union and loving affects, I am basically focused on unsettling the inherited separation of psychoanalysis as a scientific endeavor limited to the eradication of neurotic conflicts as distinct from an endeavor that also has the potential to nourish and support the powerful human need for spiritual experience and meaning. Positing the core self and focusing on its liberation from character defects and conflicts as a practice, I hope, moves us in this direction.

Duality and Unity

According to what in the West we often view as esoteric schools—
Buddhism, Taoism, Sufism, Mystical Christianity and Kabala—we as
human beings live in that which is called *the world of duality*. Duality
is considered our existential world immersion, which is largely
unconscious. In effect, it is the underlying penchant for seeing life in
black-and-white terms. Common dualistic elements we take for
granted are: us versus the other, good versus evil, right versus wrong,
pleasure versus goodness, God versus the Devil, light versus dark,
pleasure versus pain, acceptance versus fight, freedom versus
responsibility, selfishness versus unselfishness, life versus death. Life
seems to be fundamentally composed of these opposites. This way of
being in the world has a certain sort of paranoid flavor to it. It is an
orientation in which we feel fundamentally against one another and
in some ways in conflict with ourselves. We may feel we cannot accept
feelings, experiences or wishes in ourselves because they are
confirmations of some shameful experience. We cannot face ourselves
and our painful contradictory feelings so we try to be right and
righteous and deal with our self-doubts by elevating ourselves above
our faults and our neighbors and seeing life as a competition. Within
duality, competition exceeds cooperation, and being right and above
and better than the other is the highest priority. This position is a
rather ego-oriented position: ego-oriented in identification with only
ourselves, and ego-oriented in the other meaning of ego, which is a
preoccupation with self at the expense of others. It is an unconsciously
warring position with the self and others, albeit often in only
subliminal and unconscious ways.

The other way of being in the world stems from the unitive
position. The unitive state is the ultimate reality and truth, while the
world of duality is the world of illusion, which we must transcend by
way of emotional and spiritual growth. The unitive position rests in
the implicit awareness of the interconnectedness with others and all
life. It is not an elevated position of ego or self-interest, of being above
the other at all cost, and it does not deny aspects of ourselves we are
unhappy with; nor does it deny our own self-interests out of

masochistic sacrifice. Experience from within this state transcends this duality of self-care and other care, or selfishness and unselfishness. It is a rather mysterious way of living, in a sense, because laws of ethics basically fail to provide rules that can guide us through all these ethical dilemmas. It is mysterious because it is rather a felt sense of empathy with others and a connectedness to our feelings, which can resolve ethical dilemmas where outer rules fail us.

Ronald Valle (Valle & Steen, 1989), paraphrasing some of the premises of what Aldous Huxley (1970) called "perennial philosophy," developed these themes, which I believe are implicit in unitive consciousness and the nature of the core self.

1. That a transcendent, transconceptual reality or unity binds together (i.e., is immanent in) all apparently separate phenomena, whether these phenomena be physical, cognitive, emotional, intuitive or spiritual.

2. That the ego—or individualized self—is not the ground of human awareness but rather only one reflection-manifestation of a greater transpersonal (as "beyond the personal") Self or One (i.e., pure consciousness without a subject or object).

3. That each individual can directly experience this transpersonal reality that is related to the spiritual dimensions of human life.

4. That this experience represents a qualitative shift in one's mode of experiencing and involves the expansion of one's self-identity and ego self-awareness (i.e., mind is not consciousness).

5. The experience is self-validating.

Living in this unitive state as self-examination and self-transformation grow within us brings a feeling that can best be described as a sense of peace. It is a state of rest in one's feeling self that is increasingly more conflict free and less in opposition to previously warded-off aspects of ourselves, and less in opposition to others. It is the heaven that is inside us; it is Brahma; it is Nirvana. It rests in ineffable and transcendent love—a love that is not a commandment from the superego, which is not love at all, or love that is issued from the ego that knows it is simply expedient to love or at least act like you love. It is love that is a spontaneous soul movement, a love that is filled with pleasure and warmth and has its own gratification.

Spiritually oriented depth psychotherapy, with the aim of liberating the core self, can be seen as discipline that pursues this way of returning to and living from this unitive state. The depth perspective can be brought into line with this highest value again and in a more profound way than previously ever assumed. Early in his career, Freud felt that psychoanalysis was an attempt to free inhibited love and that the love he was talking about was Plato's love in the symposium. However, this idea of love seemed to become obscured in his project for a scientific psychology, his libido as discharge in accordance with the pleasure principle, his followers' use of medicalization and jargonization of his work, and his cynicism with the death instinct. Spiritually oriented depth psychology can bring back the humanistic element in Freud's depth psychology—the search for love in the soul.

In line with the unitive state is the idea that there is one instinct: the life instinct or the life force. Freud thought there were various dual instincts, although it seemed for a time he toyed with the idea of a single instinct theory. At various times he had libido in opposition to self-preservation, and then libido versus ego instincts and aggression, and finally the life instinct versus the death instinct. Interestingly enough, Freud may have been right in all cases to an extent. When we are talking on the level of duality, he is right that all these drives or instincts can be seen as opposing one another. On the unitive plane, all is one in the sense that what once was in conflict can become reconciled. Self-preservation and libido can be mutually enhancing, aggression can serve both self-preservation and preservation of the species. With the exigencies and difficulties of material life, these currents seem to get fixed into conflict. When the ego uses its faculties to transcend itself, these currents can be seen as actually enhancing one another and yoked to the same plow, as it were.

John Dorsey (1971), a student of Freud's, suggested the conflict is not really between love and hate, or love and another affective attitude, but really is the degree of consciousness of one's love—i.e., that love is the unitive source of our experience and self.

> In inhibited functioning of any kind, self love does not disappear to be supplanted by a self loveless emotion. Rather every emotion is made of nothing but love. All pathology is really physiology struggling under stressful ordeal. Anger or grief, or jealousy or whatever painful emotion is merely inhibited love struggling under stressful ordeal. Hate is hurt (hindered love), deviltry is hurt (hindered) divinity, doubt is hurt (hindered) belief, fear is hurt (hindered) safety, guilt is hurt (hindered) innocence. (p. xxxvii)

In the end, the life force of love is the only power or the only drive. Or, I should say, in the unitive state love is the only drive, and other forces such as aggression or the death drive are love's distorted derivatives. Once born into our plane of duality on this planet with the difficulties of life and its pains, the life force becomes split into opposites, and love and aggression bifurcate into the famous Freudian duality of Eros and Thanatos. Rollo May believed the life force contained potentialities for both good and evil. Carl Rogers believed that human beings' basic nature was good. Fundamentally, I do not see a contradiction between their positions. Potential for evil is within us and some of us are faced with more trauma, neglect, institutional abuse and inculcated mass pathogenic beliefs; hence the life force of love is turned into its opposite—cruelty and evil. All hostile aggression, envy and hubris and any form of cruelty constitute a permutation or deviation from love. The goal is a return to love by way of our self-examination and the ego's marriage and surrender to the universal self and life force.

The liberation of the core self through depth psychology can be understood and practiced as a transformation of duality. Even the psychoanalytic antimony of reality versus the pleasure principle is an entrapment of duality. Let me elaborate. Within the psychoanalytic framework, it is often assumed that the pleasure principle based in the unconscious simply seeks pleasure and is in total disregard of reality. On the other hand, reality is thought to be hard and delimiting and frustrating to our longings. However, as we learn about our illusions or unconscious distortions—for example, that work has to be essentially different than play—we begin to overcome this apparent dichotomy of work versus play or reality versus the pleasure principle. If we can mature to the point that we follow our heart and choose work that we enjoy, we begin to transcend this duality.

Death and Duality

There is a vast difference between hanging on to life because you fear annihilation of all you are and have become, and affirming life because you cherish the task your life on earth means.

~ Eva Pierrakos

All of our conflicts in our world of duality stem from several fundamental sources. These are: constitutional vulnerabilities to abuse, neglect and trauma; the trauma itself from various sources, especially early in life; ignorance resulting from the trauma; pathogenic beliefs of a personal or mass perspective; the common problems of living in a world where sometimes even getting our next meal can be difficult; and the universal fear of death. This fear of death is experienced by everyone on this planet, though it is often denied and disassociated with nary a conscious thought given to mortality. Others worry mightily and suffer greatly from this worry, including Freud himself. Freud had periodic bouts with death anxiety throughout his life.

Some people who may seem most "enlightened" suggest that they have the fear of death beaten. They know they will die and accept it starkly and patiently. These sorts, whom we might simply call materialists, often take this position because they feel it is "smart" not to long for something like the continuation of life. They believe it is "realistic" to even be cynical about the possibility of something beyond death or of longing for it. Those who hold this perspective are often no better off than the blind religionists who pretend they have no doubt that life is eternal and death impossible, and hold on to their faith in a rigid way, often attacking any doubts or doubters that come their way from the outside.

On a more individual level, deep in our psyche we fear that death is the model for all types of object loss, meaning loss of all our conscious experience of connection with those we hold dear. Death, then, is the model for object loss and, therefore, meaninglessness and is the anchoring point for other fears. Fear of the loss of time and the passing of time accrues from this model of loss. The fear of aging and fear of separation are two obvious examples of the attenuated fear of death.

Then we move into seemingly more subtle derivatives of the fear of death, such as loss by rejection and loss by denying someone's self-will. Deep in our psyche, when we feel denied, rejected, scorned and so forth, we equate this with death. We hold this equation because we regard our very existence as dependent upon being valued and appreciated by others. If we are not held in esteem in "their eyes," we feel we are lost to the other and abandoned—a miniature death.

When our self-will is given up, it can also be experienced as death. Self-will is the compulsion to have things go our way at all times, regardless of consequences. We often feel that our existence is predicated on holding on to things, achieving things, having things, including others' approval or attention or love, so our self-will insists that we have these gratifications. If we fail at any moment in attaining these gratifications, then the loss of gratification, things and achievements means denial of our being held in esteem in the eyes of the other—which is separation and death. Even being wrong in the most trivial of arguments can be equated with death in our unconscious, because we sometimes believe that if we are wrong we will be criticized, rejected and ostracized—which, again, is tantamount to death, albeit most often only in our subconscious. Hence, we struggle against death in daily little ways, and we struggle against life in daily little ways. When we fear death, we also become afraid to embrace life. We feel if we somehow deaden ourselves to life or avoid living fully, we can somehow protect ourselves from death. We think "it won't hurt so bad" or that we will learn how to tolerate death by suffering. So we practice suffering. In the end, though, all we do is deaden ourselves or run into suffering. In fact, deadening ourselves is suffering of a sort.

Sometimes, the fear of life can be as horrifying as the fear of death, although in the end it is merely the other side of the same coin. C.S. Lewis, the famous writer, who was an avowed atheist in his younger years, felt atheism and non-belief in an afterlife were gratifying to him at that time. He felt all that he believed in was meaningless except for his belief in atheism and the finality of death. Lewis (1955) stated:

> The materialists' world view had the enormous attraction that ... death ended all ... and if ever disasters proved greater than one wished to bear, suicide would always be possible. The horror of the Christian universe was that it had no door marked *exit* (p. 171).

Levinas, in his work on surrender, discussed a very similar state where he experienced life as horrific in a certain way with no exit. These accounts seem different than simple anxiety but contain some sort of sense of abject despair, hopelessness and meaninglessness. In his work "E&I," Levinas (1985) discusses how a relationship with another can trap us in a state he calls, with echoes of Martin Heideggar, "there is." Being trapped in "there is" invokes an abject dread of life. Levinas' remembrance of his first experience of entrapment in "there is" goes as follows:

> My reflection on this subject starts with childhood memories. One sleeps alone, the adult continues life; the child feels the silence of his bedroom as 'rumbling.' It is something resembling what one hears when one puts an empty shell up to his ear, as if the emptiness were full, as if silence were a noise... *Existence and Existents* tries to describe this horrible thing, and moreover describes it as horror and panic (p.48).

This horrific state, interestingly enough, would come to him as a child when he had trouble falling asleep. Anxiety experienced when falling asleep is often considered, in psychoanalytic circles, a type of death anxiety, but here it seems related to a life anxiety of losing oneself in being. Death anxiety and life anxiety, though different in terms of outer meaning, seem to have a common theme in this dread, horror and meaninglessness.

Levinas' entrapment in this world "there is" without a felt sense of meaning reminded me of times I had experienced something like this, a state in which all my relationships were present in my imagination but had no meaning, which was very similar to Levinas' account of his horror of meaninglessness. For me, it felt like a death anxiety as I imagined this might be what death is like, with no meaning, no connection, no felt sense that anything could matter; a black hole was the metaphor that later came to mind. Yet I recall that I had this experience where at one time I had a strong belief that life would go on for me. I felt that even my identity as an individual would carry on after death, and yet I had this same sense of inexplicable meaninglessness. In other words, if life were eternal, would there be any meaning to existence anyway, and if eternal existence was meaningless, that would really be hell. It is a rather macabre sense of things as being meaningless, or maybe because they were meaningless I felt a vague sense of horror, like a malaise that overtakes you. It was soul wrenching.

At other times, I have felt a very direct sense of death anxiety. I do believe this existential anxiety will often come to the forefront of a good and extended analysis. When this is brought out, this play of doubt and belief in psychotherapy, I believe, helps open up a felt sense of OKness with this fear, even though certainty never arrives. Somehow the horror is not so horrible and the fear is not so unbearable, even though our rational conviction may not change. Somehow this is, again, beyond any rational conviction about our fate. It is rather an emotional resettling of ourselves into a sort of trust or felt sense of the OKness of life.

Accepting the abject within us, letting go of having to be better than the next person, needing the world to do our bidding, having to be right are all little deaths that help us accept this "big death" or our struggle with non-being. Again, each time we give up our ego position of denying our faults or shortcomings, of defending our status in life or slaving for personal gain to aggrandize our ego, death becomes less frightening because it has been faced in smaller ways continuously. As this occurs, the great duality of life versus death evolves into a more unitive life and death experience.

When approached from the right way as the dying-into process, death can be likened to the process of surrender. It is a surrender to that which is unknown and abject in ourselves and also that which is extremely pleasurable, which seems to spell a loss of ego boundaries and, therefore, death itself. Anything that is abject must be accepted so as to be eventually understood and transformed into its loving origin.

The Core Self in Psychoanalytic Literature: Its Benign, Transcendent, and Ideal Dimensions

When the perceived separateness of "self" and "other" has dissolved and one's identity is secure in the spiritual Self, "being in love" becomes simply "being love." This is the realm of unconditional love, for it is only here that there is no perceived "other" to have conditions for.

~ Ronald S. Valle

This chapter has two fundamental goals: first to provide a framework for the conceptualization of a *core self* by reviewing psychoanalytic authors who hold ideas analogous to this concept; second, by using their positions as a base, to extend the concept to embrace a positive ideal dimension to the core self. By core self, I mean a self that includes self and non -self paradoxically interposed, a self or subject that is inside the other and the other inside the self. This self is also constituted by and rests in being that is a communal experience of union. Taking the positive ideals inherent in the Bionian tradition and using Plotinian philosophy as framework, I propose that this inherent communal experience or sense of union contains the positive and ideal elements of love, benevolence, capacity for concern, and all unambivalent benign aspects of human affect and experience. This self-experience embedded in communal union is the center of our being, with its array of positive, loving aspects. It is the sun behind the cloud of our defensive functioning and our negative character traits.

The classic depth psychological criticism of unitive states dwelling within the core self is that they regress to undifferentiated states, and therefore they are always pathological in nature. It is a regression to infantile states of being. Some people do regress to undifferentiation because they cannot cope with life and want to abandon their ego control over their imagination and impulses. For others, a mystical state of union is something that can be earned through spiritual development. It is a state of peace and oneness with others that is gained through having a strong and flexible ego that can be surrendered. This happens when someone has achieved psychological growth by working through the paranoid position of the ego and gained a strong desire to surrender to love for the other and life. It is a spiritual and psychological accomplishment.

Daniel Merkur (1999) champions this position:

> In developing a psychoanalytic theory of mysticism that speaks not of regression but sublimation, I have suggested that mystical moments are conscious manifestations of a general type of thinking that proceeds unconsciously. Unitive thinking may be conceptualized from a mixed Freudian and Piagetian perspective, as a category of cognitive development, akin to time perception, mathematical reasoning, and moral development. (p. ix)

The freeing and revealing of this core self from the shroud of defensive functioning could also be thought of as a liberation psychology since the goal here is ultimately the liberation of the unitive, vibrant and ecstatic core self. All the classical defenses analogously form the shroud that covers the divine self and the mantle that cloaks the pearl beyond price of Gnostic lore.

A Third Perspective[1]

Some authors, such as Winnicott (1965a, 1965b) and Kohut (1977), have emphasized the core self's inherent positive elements, but do not reflect its formal ideal aspects in the Platonic sense. Others such as Bion (1970), Grotstein (1979a, 1979b) and Eigen (1998) emphasize the core self's ideal dimension but see transcendence as a dualistic proposition: that is, comprised of both negative and positive formal ideals in the Platonic sense. I am suggesting a third view—using neo-Platonic thought to frame and affirm a position that our core selves are *ultimately* positive in the formal ideal sense, unambivalent at base, and that this can inform our clinical practice and move it in a positive transcendent direction. Grotstein's (1979a, 1979b) position seems closest to the transcendent formal elements to a core self that I am suggesting. However, his view wavers on whether the formal dimension of self is ultimately positive. At times, he infers the background object or ultimate experience is benevolent and Godlike. At other times, he suggests that a "death instinct organization" that is undifferentiated from the "life instinct organization" and the "epistemological organization" is the ultimate ground of existence, granting cruelty transcendent metaphysical properties equal to benevolence, thus asserting a dualistic ideal perspective.

This core self I am proffering—perhaps analogous to the divine spark of the Kabala—unitive at base, has to be rescued from the encumbrances of character defects and defenses to participate in the external project of liberation of others. I will suggest that the core self's interiority contains a vessel-like channel to the alterity of the other which, through felt empathy and compassion, has automatic emancipatory effects on the other.

---

[1] This section through the section ending on page 35 was excerpted from the the the article "Core Self in Psychoanalytic Literature: Its Benign and Ideal Aspects" (Sollars, 2014), originally published in the *International Journal of Behavioral Research and Psychology*. Reprinted with permission.

Paradoxical and Transcendent Elements
of the Core Self

The core self contains or expresses many paradoxes: e.g., self/non-self, fluidity/stability, interiority/exteriority, subjectivity/objectivity, multivariance/coherence, transcendence/ immanence. In attempting to understand deeper levels of being and the self, it is difficult to sum up these elements in an elegant manner. Hopefully, as I progress in reviewing theories of self that bear resemblance to the core self I postulate here, and in elucidating the paradoxes described above, an image will form that has some semblance of a pictorial contour or form that captures a good deal of the meaning the core self can metaphorically represent.

Both psychoanalytic and spiritual perspectives recognize within their traditions something analogous to the existence of a core self and, within it, a dynamic tension between intrinsic coherence and stability and firm and fluid boundaries between self and other. This paradoxical balance accounts for the characteristic transpersonal qualities of the core self. When the dualities of self and other are not denied but bridged, there is a simultaneous capacity for empathic identification and clear perspective—an ecstatic union of affect and vision that makes for a rich wisdom and ethicality. This clarity of vision permits malevolence, parochialism, selfishness, vanity and other such character-denying traits to be seen for what they are and experienced through extended identification as hurtful to the self. When real understanding and empathy are possible, appearances become less important, and rules and laws are secondary to the dictates of the heart. The other rests inside us in a felt, not intellectualized, capacity. There is an immediate awareness of our mutual identity and an empathic resonance, although they are physically separate. Referencing Meister Eckhart, Gargiulo (2004) elaborates on the notion of interiority as both exteriority and extended identification. The world exists and is constantly re-created at the edge of the me/not-me. Such internality, which Eckhart speaks of and which psychoanalysis is likewise aware of, locates the knowing other as inside the self, as well as the known-other, the world, as simultaneously internal and external (p.50).

I want to make it clear that the transpersonal position of the core self is not the same thing as a loss of self; it is not due to weak ego boundaries or to poor reality testing in an ego impaired by overwhelming negative affects or negative internalized objects. On the contrary, liberation of the core self depends on ego strength. An overwhelmed ego defends itself as long as it can and then capitulates. Only when self-defensive anxieties, impulses, and wishes have been significantly resolved can the ego surrender itself to the core self, with its firm but fluid boundaries between self and other.

Psychoanalytic Authors with Perspectives Analogous to the Core Self

Marion Milner

In her early work, Marion Milner (2011) gives play to the notion of self/non-self fluidity, considering it not as a pathological regression, but rather as a state of abundance with provisional aspects—life-affirming and restorative properties—that aid in self and object transformation (p. 188). Marion Milner was herself something of a psychoanalytic mystic who actively pursued what I am calling *spiritual goals*. She was always looking to overcome the boundaries between self and other and was able to articulate the self/other paradoxical overlap at a much earlier time than most analysts.

Mike Eigen has an illustrative take on Milner's work in his own work, *The Sensitive Self*. For Milner, a heightened sense of being spans the inner-body feel and perception of the outer world: light, color, and sound forms—the "isness" of things. Milner does not choose between the internal and external. Each may take center stage and permeate the other, contributing texture to one's creativity (Eigen, 2004c, p.39).

D.W. Winnicott

Winnicott's notion of the true self and the core self have many elements in common. Both selves have their authenticity and a seat of inspiration that belies and transcends the defensive experience of the lesser or, to Winnicott, the false self (1965b). Winnicott also suggests that the true self is fundamentally morally compassed: that is, it carries a tendency for the development of guilt and the capacity for concern (1965b, p. 25). Winnicott's concept of aggression also supports the spiritual view that the core self is ethical and benign. For Winnicott (in contradistinction to the dual instinct theory of the later Freud), aggression was not an independent instinct. Winnicott equated it with activity and the life force and considered its primary function a benign one, except to the extent that it is distorted into destruction by a less than facilitating environment. As Greenberg and Mitchell (1983) describe his view: "Aggression is a need for something in the external environment for the self to struggle with and bump up against. The aggression or 'destruction' in Winnicott's late work on object usage is thus an innocent, nonbelligerent desire for engagement," (p. 206). For Winnicott, therefore, the core self is not a dark and seething cauldron but a lively seeker of an intimate connection.

Winnicott intimates fluidity of self/non-self engagement through his concept of potential or transitional space. Transitional space is a metaphor for two simultaneous experiences, the experience of the self and the experience of evoking the other within the self. Because it is neither purely subjective nor purely objective but rather contains elements of both qualities, Winnicott recognized the transitional realm as inherently paradoxical. In his persistent focus on this paradox, he was seeking a perspective that could transcend the dichotomy between objectivity and subjectivity and honor "a third area of human living, one neither inside the individual nor outside in the world of shared reality" (1971, p. 110). Elaborating on his version of a healthy self, Winnicott states, *This is the place I have set out to examine,* the separation which is not a separation but a form of union" (p.115). Winnicott adumbrates and intimates a dual union and transcendent quality to his true self, although it is not well developed.

Christopher Bollas

Christopher Bollas is another psychoanalyst who addresses issues of similarity to the core self. Bollas speaks of the *human idiom,* which he sees as the directional compass built into our existence or the progressive articulation of the true self through the use of objects in our environment. He defines the human idiom thusly: "The idiom of a person refers to the unique nucleus of each individual, a figuration of being that is like a kernel that can, under favourable circumstances, evolve and articulate" (1989, p. 212). Throughout Bollas' writings, one can see shades of Jung, as in the articulation of the human idiom, which moves us in providential direction toward destiny. This seems to embrace elements of both Jung's self-archetype and his transcendent function. While Bollas' human idiom seems an articulation of the true self with its capacity for concern, which can be viewed as providential, it lacks much of the transcendent and transpersonal qualities of other writers such as Bion, Grotstein, Eigen, and Gargiulo.

Carl Jung

Jung's (1951) correlate of what I am calling the core self was the Self, with a capital "S." Jungian archetypes are inherited, innate, and are a priori modes of perception linked to instincts, which regulate perception and are common to all mankind. The Self is an archetype and the organizing center of the personality. It organizes, orders, and directs the personality toward self-realization. It balances the conscious and unconscious minds and is responsible for the transcendent function of harmonizing opposing trends within the personality. These opposing trends or polarizations in the personality, such as wishes for cooperation and competition, are usually considered dualities. For Jung, these dualities create a dynamic state of tension that drives the personality rather than elements—which, per force, remain debilitating by the tension they create. In Jung's ideal system, there is containment of opposites, and darkness in the personality is considered vital, something not to be eradicated by the light. While there is a "golden" element to the shadow, which, for example, can often be discovered in the darkness, much of Jung's work is a balance of the psyche, including conscious and unconscious elements, ego and shadow, and darkness and light.

Open to and influenced by the collective unconscious, which can be described as the matrix of inherited mythology and thinking processes in general, the Self archetype is deeply interconnected with others and with all of life while still maintaining its individuality. The ultimate goal of the developing personality, Jung believed, is through individuation and integration to educe and embrace the Self.

Heinz Kohut

Heinz Kohut (1984) postulated a version of the self that is analogous to the *core self,* which he called the "healthy self." Kohut posits a developmental progression in humans that proceeds toward fulfillment unless uninterrupted by traumatic experience (1971, 1984). He suggests that the healthy self, in spite of traumatic experiences, will

> mobilize its striving to complete its development, that is, that it will try again to establish an uninterrupted tension arc from basic ambitions, via basic talents and skills, towards basic ideals. The tension arc is the dynamic essence of the complete, non-defective self; it is a conceptualization of the structure whose establishment makes possible a creative-productive, fulfilling life. (1984, pp. 4–5)

As in the writings of Bollas and Jung, Kohut's view states there is a human essence that strives to be productive, creative and fulfilled. The healthy self is a structure that exists from birth—a fundamental aspect of the self, a human essence. It is sturdy and resilient and not easily subject to fragmentation or disruption. A healthy self, Kohut says,

> is a structure that—except perhaps as an outcome of the most severe forms of traumatization such as prolonged confinement in concentration camps and other protracted dehumanizing experiences—is not prone to become fragmented, or disharmonious during maturity, at least not severely and/or for long periods of time. (Kohut 1984, p. 70)

Kohut's notion of a healthy self contains the idea of a fluid and empathic boundary between self and other. Speaking of analysis and the liberation of the healthy self states, Kohut (1984) says:

> the third step—the essential one because it defines the aim and the result of the cure—is the opening of a path of empathy between self and object, specifically the establishment of empathic in-tuneness between self and self object on a mature adult level. This new channel of empathy permanently takes the place of the formerly repressed or split-off archaic narcissistic relationship. (pp. 65–66)

Kohut also terms his healthy self *the nuclear self,* which serves to situate the self centrally in his psychic system. Its movement toward a creative, productive and fulfilling life provides a providential element to his notion of self. His notion of healthy narcissistic development, which leads to a fulfilling life unless interrupted by trauma, also results in powerful empathic attunement and appreciation of the other, which touches an unsettling of the self/other dichotomy. However, it is not strong in this regard and does not see the other in the self and the self in the other in such a radical way as Bion, Gargiulo, Eigen, and myself.

Bion's Platonic Idealism and His Psychoanalytic Lineage

It is my belief that the "transcendent position" represents the achievement of the state of meditative-like grace in which one experiences solitude with a serenity that transcends conflict.

~ *James Grotstein*

Wilfred Bion

Wilfred Bion (1963, 1965, 1970), one of psychoanalysis' most novel and extraordinary thinkers, provided a new metapsychology for psychoanalysis. He integrated and condensed (some may say conflated) Kant's *thing in itself*, Plato's *concept of the forms*, and an ideal conception of God through the deification of the two former theoretical positions.

For purposes of explanation, Immanuel Kant, perhaps the greatest philosopher of at least recent past, asserted that there is an inner mind-dependent realm of being that he called *phenomena*. He also believed there is an outer world that could be represented in our mind but could never be actually known. Things in the outside world are transcendental objects, or *noumena.*

Plato, the ancient Greek philosopher, believed in an ideal world, or *world of forms*, that had a greater reality than the material world of appearance. Plato's world of forms was the causal world, human beings' ideas, with material objects sort of transduced or brought into being from this causal world of greater mind and forms. For Plato, in some sense there is never anything new under the sun, but new creations and things are materializations of the world of ideas or forms. A chair, for example, becomes a chair because it has the formal properties of a chair that were transduced from the world of mind—four legs, a place to sit on, and a back to lean against.

Wilfred Bion seemed to embrace both of these philosophical elements in his conceptualization of beta elements or preexistent thoughts and originary experience, which is the realm in which the beta elements exist. This originary experience, a neologism, Bion represents with the capital letter "O." Much of his theory relates to the containment of preexistent elements or the rejection of them from our conscious experience. "O" has both a transcendent dimension and an immanent, panentheistic dimension. "O" is ubiquitous within, through and around us. Bion's famous rendezvous with "O" connects us with the Godhead in its transcendence and the "other" in a panentheistic embrace of the immanent.

In contrast to our ego, which may possess "K" or *knowledge* about "O," "F" or *faith* in "O" is required for "O's" embrace. In faith, "O" can be experienced as thoughts without a thinker and without shattering the containing and non-impeding self. Understanding "O" through rational functions is for Bion always a myth or falsity that impedes "truth" in "O" in both its transcendence and immanence. Grotstein

(1981), referencing Bion, suggests the "O" that faith embraces is "our Truing 'O' which must, through us, constantly intersect with its counterpart, the 'O' of the Other" (p.55).

I believe this notion that the experience of "O" within us constantly intersects with the "O" of the other unsettles the subject/object, interior/exterior, and self/other dichotomies and speaks of shared originary experience within and between all of us. It speaks of an inherent unity we all share that can be recognized as inherent in the conception of the core self. Bion (1970) in his later work equated the originary experience of "O" with the ideal of the Godhead. Forsaking the "miscreant container" or the ego as the expression of the ultimate self, he thought of the self more as the background originary subject/object of experience. The self seemed transcendent.

Grotstein on Bion states: "'I'ness consists, furthermore in a prismatic refraction of the emanations of this Godhead..." (Grotstein, 1981, p. 505). The notion of "prismatic refractions" in relation to Bion's thought strongly resembles Plotinus' Emanations from the One, the Monad, or the divine.

James Grotstein

James Grotstein (1979a, 1979b, 1981, 1998, 2000a, 2000b) is one of Wilfred Bion's foremost students and translators. Like any good student, he extended some of his teacher's ideas while challenging others. Grotstein embraces Bion's Platonism, but he places emphasis on the ineffable subject, *the Dreamer*, who "dreams the dream." The ineffable subject, the dreamer of dreams, is always subjective and never objectively experienced. While an eminent authority on Melanie Klein, Grotstein spoke directly of Platonism in his work, as well as Gnosticism, the Kabala, and mysticism: "I conceive of the Subject as being both *numinous* or *ineffable*, as the Subject of subjects, not unlike the Gnostic sense of the 'God' within us..." (Grotstein, 1998, p.43). In the same paper, he wrote:

> It has become my growing impression that religion, spirituality, and mysticism, the channels by which human

beings seek to consult their gods, the God-lore altogether, have been ways since time immemorial that human beings have attempted to divine the numinous, the ineffable within them, the Subject, or really, the *Subject of Subjects*, if I may express it in the way of the mystics (Grotstein, 1998, p.45).

Fascinating in both his depth and breadth of work, Grotstein has made a place for mysticism and spirituality in depth psychology. Perhaps only Wilfred Bion and Carl Jung exceed him in paving a way for a depth psychological conception and practice of spirituality.

Michael Eigen

Michael Eigen (1983, 1995, 1998, 2004a, 2004b, 2004c), a prolific writer and psychoanalytic mystic, is another in the line of Bion who speaks of the raw experience of "O" in both its ideal splendorous and horrific forms. Eigen (1983) also references a dual-track self. He offers the term *dual union* to refer to the simultaneous presence of these two aspects of the self/other experience—the experience of distinction and the experience of union. Eigen believes that this basic experiential structure of dual union is characteristic of the self across all of its developmental levels.

Therefore, neither separateness nor union is a bedrock construct of human experience. It is perhaps more appropriate to speak of a two-in-oneness or one-in-twoness. Pure merger and isolation are abstract terms that do not characterize living experience. Areas of union and distinction occur together, with one or the other emphasized more in a given situation. In this context, Christian conceptions of a triune God or communion (co-union) appear to reflect a genuine advance in mystical and psychological description. Here a sense of division and union coexist fully, neither being possible without the other. Whatever its theological function, this kind of formulation expresses the basic structural requirements that a theory of the self (or ego) must meet (Eigen, 1983, pp. 423–424).

In this later work, Eigen (2004c) also points to a transcendent ideal aspect of the self, which is unambivalent, pure and beatific at the heart of the self:

> Yet something claws at the innards, a vision. Radiance. Light.
> There does seem to be something unambivalent at the core—
> perhaps what is meant by calling the soul pure. For example,
> mystical Judaism affirms there is a point of the soul ever pure
> in contact with God. This, even though the empirical self or
> soul is quite impure (p. 166).

Thus, Eigen not only begins to embrace a notion of unambivalence and
purity, he places it precisely at our deepest center and uses "core" as
the analogy.

While Eigen never gives up the play of dualistic elements such as
love/brokenness, devil/angel, deadness/aliveness and so forth, his
work has culminated in a full embrace of the mystical elements of the
Kabala. In *Kabbalah and Psychoanalysis* (2013), he talks in depth of
Bion's indebtedness to the Kabala and how the Kabala's mysticism,
including *Ein Soph* or ineffable God, and the *Sepherot* tree, or divine
cosmological plan that moves creation, are also elements of each
individual in the here and now.

Monad and the Unity of "O"

> *"I am striving to give back the Divine in myself to the Divine
> in the All."*
>
> ~ *Plotinus*

I would like to suggest an even more ambitious ideal for the
psychoanalytic project, rather than containment of the array of forms
from the horrific to the sublime. I suggest the goal could be the
discovery within each of us of the ideal positive aspects of "O" which,
I submit, always lie waiting for liberation from within any negative
experience of "O." My proposition is that the ultimate "O" is the ideal
"O" that is in close proximity to the divine, as Plotinus (Armstrong,
1962) might suggest. Plotinus was one of the major philosophers of
the ancient world, a translator of Plato and perhaps the foremost Neo-
Platonic thinker. (I wish to reiterate here that the psychoanalytic tree

of Bion, Grotstein, Eigen and others of this group, in my opinion, have Platonism embedded in their metapsychology.) The ultimate truth and metaphysical existence for Plotinus is the divinity of the Monad or Godhead, and our world or experience of appearances is just a distortion. Plotinus believed we actually live Plato's allegory of the cave and only see the sun's reflection on its wall. The sun is the Godhead, and we have a great deal of difficulty believing in its reality, instead seeing mostly its shadow. The shadow here is the negative experience (appearance) of projected hate, envy and greed that accrues from character defenses that shroud the Monad and benevolent, peaceful existence.

Plotinus

For Plotinus, Plato's formalistic idealism begins in the one, or Monad, although to say "begins" is already a distortion since it is beyond time and causality. The Monad is the Divine essence of all. It is perfect in love and wisdom and unites everything and everyone. Plotinus speaks of emanations, which can be thought of as the Monad's diffusion of itself. That is, the further away from the source emanations devolve the more distortion there is—i.e., the less divine and the more negative. Thus, horrific forms of experience can be thought of as having separated out as emanations from the source of the Monad and perturbed into more negative forms. In my estimation, the horrific forms of malevolence and cruelty are abjectly separated and distorted forms of the Monad. Ultimate, unambivalent, divine "O," analogous to the Godhead, on the other hand, rests within the "heart" or deeper psyche of all of us.

Psychoanalysis can aid in the reclamation of the "Original 'O'" of the Monad from the dualistic perturbation of "O" into more negative forms. Thus, the ultimate aim of psychoanalysis from this perspective is not merely the containment of both good and bad ideals of distorted forms, but the transformation of the negative back into positive. Hate, for example, can be seen as love outraged. Envy can be a distortion of admiration, hubris a distortion of self-esteem and so forth. For Plotinus, the individual soul is a lower irradiation of the divine, but as such contains a trace of the divine that holistically contains all of the divine. Hence, herein lies my equation of the core self with the Kabala's notion of the *divine spark of the soul* and the Gnostic's *pearl beyond price.*

The soul's ultimate reality is unambivalent, sublime and connected with the Monad. It is that which understands our inherent innersubjective connection to the other and the "All" and experiences this truth, albeit mostly unconsciously. If we can experience the light of the unambivalent sublime, contain it and not shrink from it, we can transcend the world of appearances ("the lie") and experience the Monad's inherent love and ecstatic relational capacities embedded in what is analogous to the core self of our being.

I would like to take a second to comment on the self/no-self experience that some find in contradiction to the core self's *self/other experience of union.* In my estimation, when mystics experience the bliss of no-self experiences, they are really experiencing the caesura of consciousness that allows the bliss of the unambivalent "0" or Monad to reach them. The open space allows the blissful forms of peace and the surrender to the Allness of others and life to occur. As much fullness as emptiness occurs, but the fullness/emptiness paradox is very hard to describe. Gargiulo (2004) speaks of the mist of infinite possibilities that fill the emptiness. The core self that I wish to speak of is at one with these sublime forms and, in some way, partakes of their essence. Two elements are one on this level of being. This is the area of communion or "at one-ness" with the *other* and the "All" that is sought after in various mystical schools. Some think this union is a function of no-self, but I suggest that it is a uniting of self and other, or rather the embrace of the place where self and other are already united deep within our psyche. This *caesura* is the place where faults such as envy, hubris, spite do not hold sway and keep us from the experience of union. This place can be found, at times, through meditation and also through transcendent experiences of union in psychoanalysis, as character faults that shroud the core self are worked through.

We find the other through our interiority. We find the other through the embrace of our character defenses and faults and ultimately the joy and love that lies waiting and underpins all that we are. The more we can experience our malevolence or spite or any negative character trait fully and without defense and still keep our eye on the prize of our loving core self within, the nearer we are to our divinity. Hate is love outraged, and fear is a separation from union. "The darker the devil the brighter the angel" is an old Kabalistic expression. It can be true in the work of psychoanalysis as well.

In "Instincts and their Vicissitudes," Freud (1915) spoke of the reversal of love into hate. "The change of the content of an instinct into its opposite is observed in a single instance only—the transformation of *love into hate*" (p.133). In an effort to preserve his dual instinct theory, Freud quickly suggested that hate is derived from the *self's* preservative instinct, asserting that it is of different origin than love born from libido. At the level of the ideal, unambivalent core, self-aggression is always a derivation of love. In Winnicottian terms, "an innocent, nonbelligerent desire for engagement" (Winnicott, 1965). Any character fault or malevolent feeling is a distortion and permutation of a benign ideal form. The understanding that in any experience of the abject or malevolent within us, the core self is available underneath and within the fault is an important factor. It can buoy us against the self-hate that accrues from the negative affect and character faults. It also helps us keep our eye on the prize of the unfolding of our positive human nature.

Those of the Bionian tradition emphasize the containment of projections and beta elements and, finally, faith in the embrace of raw experiences of "O" in both their negative and positive forms. In this thesis, I contend that in any "dark" experience of "O," a positive experience awaits liberation. The negative experiences of "O" are simply the dark night of the soul that is a preamble to the dawn of something positive emerging from darkness. Other authors cited in this thesis also suggest that our deepest nature is relational, positive, and morally compassed. Winnicott, Kohut, Bollas, and Jung all postulate concepts analogous to a positive core self. However, their ideal dimension is not informed by the transcendence of Platonic formalism.

Bionians influenced by the Platonic tradition challenge the darkness of our human nature more directly, but seem to stop there with a sort of equivalence in the containment of positive and negative aspects of "O." I am suggesting that we go through the negative by way of embracing the negative, but that we look for the liberation of positive affects and experience from the darkness of our psyche. I am suggesting that the positive is always inherent in the negative, but the question is whether or not it is found. Do we continue to live the illusion of the shadows on the wall of the cave, or do we see the reality of the light?

The One and the Many

Jeffrey Rubin (1999) emphasizes the non-self aspects of the self/non-self paradox. He does not entirely repudiate the fixed or coherent facets of selfhood, but he values and concentrates on the fluid aspects of the self: "Psychoanalysis needs different theories of self-theories that elude reifying and reductionistic trends; that value emergent and evolving as well as fixed and determinate facets of selfhood; and that are polyphonic or many-sided, rather than monological or one dimensional" (p. 153). He discusses a *non-self-centered subjectivity* that is reminiscent of what I am calling *the fluidness of the core self's boundaries*:

> Non-self-centered subjectivity . . . is a psychological/spiritual phenomenon implicated in a wide range of adaptive behaviors ranging from art to psychoanalytic listening to intimacy. It is an unconstricted state of being, a non-self-preoccupied, non-self-annulling immersion in whatever one is presently doing in which there is heightened attentiveness, focus, and clarity. Action and response are unconstrained by self-concern, thought, or conscious effort, and restrictive self-identifications and boundaries are eroded (p. 118).

While privileging the multidimensionality of the self and non-self-centered subjectivity, the coherence and consistency of the concept of something akin to the core self is, for Rubin, sometimes thought of despairingly as stultifying to growth and creating a Procrustean bed that requires painful conformity. In Rubin's view, Winnicott's conception of a True Self is simply a reification of a myth and, perhaps, ironically false. In contradistinction to Rubin, in this author's opinion the True Self is a characterization of a phenomenologically real self-state. It is real in terms of a psychic system or structure while not having material reality, which Rubin would rightfully consider reification. Rubin's self is complex and uncentered, but still existent. He actually offers the term *core self* as a non-essentialistic description of a multidimensional self. Rubin's sense of the core self, while having some similarities with the core self I proffer, represents the non-distinction side of the distinction/non-distinction paradox. The core self I am postulating emphasizes distinction and coherence more than Rubin's. Additionally, it has transcendent formal aspects that have essentialist elements.

Bromberg (1996) and Davies (1998) focus on multiple self states and, much like Milton Erickson (1976), see trance states and dissociations as much more common than most psychotherapists acknowledge. This has a great deal of merit and is reminiscent of Robert Assagioli's (2000) subpersonalities. Subpersonalities, or multiple self-states, are split off and dissociated aspects of the self with their own intentionalities. For Assagioli, the integration of these subpersonalities into an integral whole is an important aspect of his work. Bromberg (1996) and Davies (1998) seem to deemphasize integration of these self-states and believe no one particular self-state should be privileged over the other. I do believe we have to be careful about privileging more benevolent elements of the personality in concern that more abject elements of the personality will be dissociated. Having said that, it seems important to note that integration of these more conflictual elements of the personality into less conflictual and benevolent elements is something implicitly available in Bromberg's work. In discussing the movement from greater conflict to lesser conflict by way of his psychoanalytic work, Bromberg states:

> And so it went, with his becoming more and more able to hold in a single state of consciousness, without dissociation, complex interpersonal events that contained

feelings toward another person that formerly would have collided traumatically and thus would have been too incompatible with his ongoing self-definition to allow self-reflectiveness and the experience of resolvable intrapsychic conflict (p. 517).

As with Assagioli's work and Jung's transcendent function, there is a higher order integrative property within us. Its arch is toward integration and harmonization of these subpersonalities or split off aspects of ourselves that create conflict. Sometimes these multiple self-states are repressed, sometimes dissociated and sometimes consciously accepted and remain syntonic while their conflictual aspects are ignored. As integration of these states proceeds, conflict between subpersonalities inexorably gives way to greater harmony and unification while paradoxically retaining the possibility of conscious, healthy expression of variety and complexity in the personality.

Multiple self states and subpersonalities articulate the fact that we all have various aspects to ourselves that, at times, seem to function orthogonally. "All the world's a stage" and we have a cast of characters within us that vie for a role on that stage. These multifaceted aspects of ourselves describe elements of pathology and also the normative richness of who we are. However, we are also *one* as well as many. There is an organizing integrative and integrated aspect to who we are that is foundational. It has many outpicturings, much as a precious gem often has many sides that refract and reflect the light shined upon it. The core self is a gem, the *pearl beyond price*. Its transcendent benevolent properties underlie the many facets of our personality that seek expression as either a creative or problematic way of adapting to life.

Mystical Religious and Spiritual Traditions
with Positions Analogous to the Core Self

For students really interested in comparative perspectives on mysticism, spirituality and religion, a rich platform to explore these ideas can be found in the scholarly writings of William James (2008), Evelyn Underhill (1911) and Wainwright (2007). Of course, a lifetime of study could be devoted to each religious perspective and one would still have a lot to learn. For the purposes of this book, I will outline mystical traditions in major religious movements that speak of what I refer to as the core self. I will not attempt a comprehensive review of their positions, which have an analogous version of the core self, but I will provide enough of a brief sketch to point out the rather historic fact that the core self's liberation has been sought since axial time and perhaps earlier.

In contemporary popular thought, the core of the self is often referred to as *the Higher Self*. The Higher Self is discovered or uncovered in many ways, including meditation and prayer, and some schools also use depth psychological work. The Pathwork of Self Transformation, founded on the teachings of Eva Pierrakos (2012), is one such school that employs depth work to spiritual transformation as well as prayer, meditation and self-examination.

In mystical Christianity, especially Gnostic Christianity, the Core of each of us is the divine spark. The divine spark is a fragment of divinity that is scattered due to the fall of the angels. Each created and fallen being, which includes human beings, contains such a divine spark that must be reintegrated into the greater divinity. The low self shrouds the spark. The myth of the Pearl captures this notion, as the Pearl is the divine spark for which we have to dive into our lower elements to bring back to the surface or light. Practices often include prayer, study of scripture, devotion and meditation. Retrospective mediation examines how one was reactive and behaved poorly or let his or her emotions get out of hand. With retrospective review, alternative ways of being and behaving are visualized to shape future behavior, thoughts and feelings in a positive direction.

Christian Kabala has the same divine spark and higher self that you will find in the Jewish version of Kabala, but Christ's role in the plan of salvation and the tree of life is more centrally located. In other forms of Christian mysticism, such as we find in St. John of the Cross and Sister Teresa Ávila, it may be referred to as the *indwelling presence* of God or Christ. Although the Christian doctrine of original sin may be seen to contradict the notion of a core self or higher self, in the Christian Kabala the original sin refers to the cosmological fall from grace by eating from the tree of knowledge, not the ultimate or original state of the soul.

Ancient Jewish Mysticism and the Kabala also use the concept of divine sparks as personality fragments that must be reintegrated into the whole of the divine. This requires both self-facing and surrender. Historically, the Torah is studied, as well as an immersion in the oral traditions.   Prayer, meditation, self-examination and even numerology have been applied to help the soul in its upward journey on the *Sephiroth*, or tree of life. The Book of Splendor, or *The Zohar*, originally published by Moses de Leon in the thirteenth century and attributed to the channeling of the Prophet Elijah by Rabbi Shimon Bar Yochai, is a major element of the oral tradition of the Kabala.

In Hinduism the Atman has some measure of equivalence to the core self I proffer. The Atman is often considered fused with the Brahman. At other times the Brahman retains a distinction as a true self somehow different than the Atman, thus expressing the distinction–union paradox. The Atman always remains the eternal core of the human being rather than persona or outer expression of the personality. Common practices that are used to uncover the core self are meditation, yoga, contemplation of the divine and self denial.

Buddhism's version of the core self is often called *the greater self.* It is the self that is identified with the suffering of others and contains the moral aim of helping others. Another term for the core self is the *Buddha nature,* which is also called the greater self. The greater self is often contrasted with the lesser self, with its traits of vanity, self-interest or egotism.

The issue of an essential self versus a nonessential self has perplexed many adherents of Buddhism for centuries. The Buddha himself was asked if there was an eternal essential self or ultimately no self. As the story goes, he refused to answer. When later asked why, he said, "to hold either that there is a self or that there is no self is to fall into extreme forms of wrong view that make the path of Buddhist practice impossible." For this author, Buddha's no self is coextensive with no ego, or elevated self-interest, not loss of the personality. The idea of the Buddha positing a radical version of no self, no identity, doesn't fit with related ideas in the sutras of the soul transmigrating through various lifetimes. That the Buddha nature contains an essential core self, while paradoxically in constant flux and development in terms of letting go of separateness and ego elevation, fits perfectly with a consistent understanding of the texts.

Buddhist's spiritual practices include meditation and the application of Buddhist scripture or Sutras to everyday life. A major emphasis is placed on the application of the four noble truths and the eightfold noble path. The noble truths contain the fundamental philosophical conception that life is hard, and accepting life's hardship without railing against this fundamental fact begins a path of liberation. The eightfold noble path is focused on practicing right actions, right thinking, right intention, right view and so forth.

The mystical school within Islam is the sect of Sufism. Sufis embrace the concept of the higher self, which contains a unity with the divine and a compassionate identification with the suffering of others. Sufis work with the inner self and its problematic elements, including lower self or dark elements, to liberate the higher self within us. They often use prayer, devotion, self-examination and study of scripture to identify lower self elements and free the higher self from egoistic encumbrances.

Taoists use the term *Higher Self* or *Golden Body* to refer to the spiritual self in contact with the divine that also contains a distinction–union dimension. Common spiritual practices that are used to wake the higher self from its sleep are meditation, martial arts such as Tai Chi, diet restrictions, especially the avoidance of alcohol and meat, breathing exercises and the avoidance of negative emotions such as greed, pride, lust, anger and vanity.

As the brief outline I provided above shows, the conception of a core self in slumber or shrouded by encumbrances, waiting to be liberated, has been present since axial time in the history of the major religions' more mystical schools, and front and center in many Eastern religions such as Hinduism, Buddhism and Taoism. In this text, I point the reader to the use of depth psychology as an accelerated method of liberating the core self from the encumbrances of character faults, pain, fear and separation from others by way of the paranoid position of the ego.

Chapter 2
The Model

My intention in this chapter is to suggest a model that might be useful to conceptualize the alchemical process of transforming duality to unity and negative character traits to loving capacities and expanded identity. There are other models to conceptualize this process, but I have found this one very useful. I want to make clear that the model is not entirely unique. It closely resembles what can be found in the lectures of Eva Pierrakos (2012); however, I come to the material rather differently, from a psychoanalytic perspective. You may see echoes of Robert Assagioli's psychosynthesis, the Buddha nature hidden beneath the five hindrances, Plotinus' formulation of the Monad and its emanations into the darkness of lower worlds, and many others. Rather than a completely new theory, it is an extension and perhaps interpretation of already existent world views that I have simply tried to bring into a clear focus as a model. A major difference, however, which is what this text is about, is the application of a depth psychological approach to spiritual transformation—an approach that is perhaps either too thinly expressed or not found at all in these other worldviews.

Personality Diagrammatically

To paint a picture of the personality theory I am suggesting, I use the cosmic egg with four different self elements represented within. The core self, illustrated by the iridescent yellow, is the deepest level of our personality. Faintly displayed within the core self is the most recognizable symbol of unitive consciousness, the Taoist Yin Yang. The core self is permeably shrouded by the lower self, represented by the center portion of the egg. The lower self contains the character

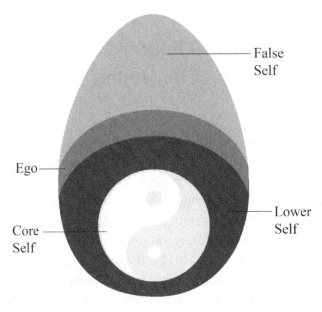

Artwork by Janis Glotkowski, MA, TLLP

Core Self, Lower Self, Ego, and False Self

faults, conscious and unconscious negativity, and negative inner will. The ego represented by the darker grey in the middle portion of the egg shrouds both the lower self and core, yet is sometimes part of the lower self when self-identification involves being against others. The ego has decision-making functions and commonly understood capacities such as judgment, discernment and will. The ego is in the position of deciding whether to align with the core self or fight against it and the world. The ego is often deeply afraid of both lower self and the core self, fearing the eruption or the expression of the shadow elements of the personality with the problems they cause. The ego equally fears the core self and its own greatness because of its melting, loving and ecstatic unitive qualities that recognize others around us as equal to us in a very real felt sense. The false self represented by the lighter grey near the point of of the egg shrouds the ego, the lower self and the core. The false self presents a facade to the world. It is an outpicturing of what it thinks is the best image it can present based on inner fears and aggression. It pretends to be an ideal of what it should be, to ingratiate itself to others or elicit obeisance and deference from others. This false-self presentation may often be at the expense of the person's inner integrity and deeper values and alienates the person from his or her deeper self.

The work, from this perspective, is to transform the masks and pretenses of the false self, the ego's identification with separateness and apostatizing of reason, and the hostility, ignorance and character faults of the lower self back into the pure gold of the core self. All negative character traits and pretenses are ultimately distortions of the loving expression of the core self. They are *love outraged*. Once understood and worked through, they eventually revert back to loving qualities through the alchemical process of transformation.

Freud's model is the tripartite structural model of id, ego and superego. The id contains the instincts including sex, aggression and self-preservation, or the death instinct, depending on whether you are reading early Freud or late Freud. The ego, in touch with reality, must manage impulses from both the id and the superego, which can become cruel itself. In the Freudian model, the goal is for ego management and modulation and control of the impulses and structures.

In this more spiritual/mystical model, the inner spiritual self or *Core Self* rests in the unitive state, which is beyond the structures delineated by Freud. The core is the self that is peaceful, loving, creative, outpouring and wise. Through the difficulties of our development, many life-denying institutions, and even constitutional problems we may be born with, our spiritual, spontaneous, vital self in measure becomes deadened and defended against. The desire for love in all its permutations may become subverted and displaced or converted into its opposites. The better the individual parenting that we experience in our development, and by the community, the more our loving qualities are not deadened and distorted but remain outpouring and outreaching.

The Lower Self
The aspect of our personality that becomes distorted and misdirected so that love in various ways becomes permutated into hate, avarice,

cruelty or envy may be called what is popularly known as *the shadow* or, in some esoteric schools, *the lower self*. This would be closest to Freud's id or Jung's shadow, although the lower self has what would seem to be more of an intentional consciousness while Freud's id is merely raw, primitive instincts. Jung introduced the term *shadow* into popular parlance, and it refers to aspects of ourselves of which we are unaware and which are most often negative. The shadow's negative elements, I would say, can be defined as being against the best interest and well-being of others and ourselves.

All of our childhood hurts, troubles and life hurdles cause psychic pain. They cause hurt and dysphoric feelings of many types, including guilt and shame. These hurts cause the child's loving current to be outraged. This outrage can morph into all kinds of negative feelings, defenses and character faults such as greed, envy, spite, jealousy, entitlement, and cruelty. Any form of malevolence that we might call the low self or shadow is love outraged. This outraged love in distortion ultimately constitutes our lower self. However, since the lower self is love outraged, it points to the possibility that these negative character traits can be converted back into loving, caring feelings and traits—core self elements.

James Grotstein (1979) describes a phenomenon akin to this low-self element. He calls it *the magus object*. This is an internal object or aspect of self-functioning that actually seeks to destroy goodness in the self and the world. Based on paranoid projection of its own malevolence and ill will, it feels goodness is not real and that benevolence in the world is actually a trap meant to enslave us. Therefore, it cannot trust love, relationships or happiness, as happiness is a herald of manipulation and exploitation by others. This magus object works like a cabal rather than an indiscriminant, unorganized impulse. Grotstein's formulation is analogous to what I think the low self to be. In an organized fashion, sometimes conscious but often unconscious, it actually works against maturity, growth, love and benevolence because it just does not trust them. This low-self shroud, which covers the core self, has to be analyzed and worked through to liberate the core self with its love, benevolence and wisdom. Not just envy and projected hostility, but all character faults such as greed, spite, avarice, and hubris are the elements that compose the low self, along with its organized, negative intentionality.

Plotinus' conception is that we have a higher and lower soul. The higher soul has some remembrance of the divine while the lower is separated off further from the One and has fallen into vices, character faults and destructive passions. The higher soul is involved in shepherding this lower soul back to unity with the One—the Divine. The low self is embedded in our materialistic, dualistic, worldly winds.

Michael Eigen's (2004b) *The Psychotic Core*, I believe, can be equated with our lower self. The psychotic core represents the dark, anti-life, intentionally negative, often cruel and always ignorant aspects of ourselves that substantiate our lower self. When the mask of pretense and false self is examined, an often passionate, unconscious, negative intentionality becomes conscious, and then it is up to the deciding conscious elements of our consciousness, or ego, that must make the decision to challenge or go with the negative intentionality of the lower self.

Roberto Assagioli (2000) uses a conception of the low self in his psychosynthesis model. He postulates that the lower unconscious is split off from what he calls the higher self and fragmented into subpersonalities. This is similar to what I am suggesting. But Assagioli does not emphasize the shrouding of the higher self with negative character traits as occurs with the lower self, which also has conscious elements to it as well as unconscious. In addition, his techniques are quite different than the depth psychological approach I am advocating in that they don't go right after the lower self with its passions and guilt, which are often, but not exclusively, situated in the unconscious. When the depths of a person's "demons" are not approached rigorously in this way, it often leads to a false sense of inflation in which people identify with those aspects of themselves that are already transformed. This causes a false sense of security and peace until the worldly winds of life reach out and unsettle the false sense of ourselves and our brittle peace.

The Ego, Its Elements and Vicissitudes

Freud's original term for the ego was the "I," or the sense of oneself that is conscious and knowable. Those elements that were foreign and unconscious or outside of awareness were called the "It." The "It" was that which came to our minds from outside, as it were, impeding what we know of as "I," or ourselves. The concepts of "I" and "It" later were Latinized by Freud's major interpreter, James Strachey, and some of his other followers. The "I" became the ego, and the "It" became the Id. Many believe the Latinization and medicalization of Freud's terms were an effort to make psychoanalysis less pedestrian and place it outside of popular knowledge. Later, what Freud termed the "Over I," or the part of our minds that looks down on us, so to speak, and evaluates us morally, became the superego.

Hence, the "I" turned ego is another term for the self in Freudian psychology. It has administrative functions, though, and among these are judgment, discrimination, adapting to reality, synthesizing internal drives and feelings with external reality, and tolerance of feelings and frustration. The ego tries to cope with and adapt to reality and tries to master and cope with internal drives and feelings of the id. The ego, in this sense, is largely in opposition to the id, and its best hope is a measure of compromise and mastery over the id.

From a spiritual point of view, the ego and its ultimate fate can be looked at a little differently. The ego is an extension of our involuntary feeling self. It grows out of this nascent self when the frustrations of life begin to cause us to need to delay our wishes and think about new ways to obtain what we long for. It is not absolutely different from our feeling, involuntary intuitive self, but experientially it does become differentiated out of the involuntary feeling self-matrix. It rises up to take its place in the world to manage life and define itself and its needs. At some point in our individual development and perhaps in history, it comes in conflict with our instinctual life and our passions. Many aspects of religion have evolved, in some sense, to let our rational self take greater control of our instincts and help the individual become master of him- or herself and his or her impulses. Freud himself believed that logic and reason, and their ability to manage impulses, were the only thing that could save humanity.

While we do have base instincts and need to control these instincts, both on the individual and societal level, it can be seen that there is a life-affirming alternative—an alternative in which surrender to the lifestream, a dying into the greater self of life and the involuntary, can be felt to be even more expansive, liberating and peace inducing than ego mastery and control. The alternative is a place—which you might say is more vital than intellectual or willful ego control, more intuitive and wise than ego logic—that reconciles many apparently conflicting decisions that are impossible to resolve adequately when the outer ego is relied on for all decisions. It is a place of surrender of the ego to our involuntary real self and the lifestream. It is a place where the ego seeks the guidance from our inner wisdom, which is connected to the lifestream of love. The ego here is not forsaken but provided its rightful place as subordinate to the life lived from the passionate wisdom and the creative, intuitive core self within. Just as outer logic and deductive reasoning often need to be subordinated to intuition, if life is to be spontaneous and meaningful, a strong ego is needed—not as the final measure of health or spiritual development but so that it can surrender itself to the real self and lifestream within.

Weak Ego. When the ego is too weak, feelings threaten to override the control and balance in the personality. Feelings then cannot be contained and used for both their wisdom and information. Real feelings are manifestations of the inner real or vaster core self that is connected with the life force. This life force has an intelligence to it that exceeds our ego's attempts to manage life. In the end, the life force is love, and any other feelings that are not life affirming are real feelings that have deviated from their origin in love and have become negative and destructive because of trauma, the pains of life and our own ignorance.

Strong Ego. Developing a strong ego is sort of a halfway point in this model. The ego must be able to contain feelings and examine them for their underlying meaning to eventually transform them back into a more loving state. To do this, the ego must be strong and resilient, meaning that it must be able to accept unflattering desires and wishes and experiences into awareness to undo repression and allow for a mourning and transformation of these unwanted wishes and experiences.

For example, a woman may hate men categorically but deny it because it is unflattering, and then project this sentiment and think all men are jerks and out to treat her badly and exploit her. After self-examination, she may find that she really is angry at men and chooses "jerks" who confirm her anger so she just does not have to face her anger. Then she may subsequently find that under her anger is a strong longing for men that she has to deny because in her childhood her father was both unavailable and rejecting. After examining herself and realizing how she is externalizing blame for her troubles to others, she is left with a longing for men that she may now believe is safe to feel, which allows, finally, for a productive relationship. The negative feelings must first be held by the ego into consciousness so that the original longing and hurt can be bared and mourned, which then allows the more basic desire for love and longing to emerge. The ego has to be strong enough to perform this operation so that the woman can surrender to more loving and life-affirming feelings. This, eventually, is a state the ego does not have to control. When she was in her more negative state, her ego may have had to use repression or other defense mechanisms to control her anger at men because those feelings may have threatened both her self-esteem and need for safety. After she has contained and worked through these negative feelings, the ego can relax into a loving state more easily.

Rigid Ego. When the ego is too tight or over controlled, it is a problem too. If the ego is rigid and defends against unconscious negativity with too much repression, then the negative affect will always threaten to break through and cause anxiety or other neurotic symptoms or worse. This overcontrol can lead to so many problems, from someone being a rather desiccated intellectual to paranoia. Sometimes drugs and other types of compulsions and addictions as well as psychosomatic problems are used as releases from this over-tight ego control. Only a strong and flexible ego is able to move from repressing negative feelings to containing them in consciousness and transforming them by understanding their source as love outraged at the core.

The ego at base is an aspect of the universal self that was once congruent with the lifestream and our involuntary processes, and was then differentiated out of those involuntary processes. This progression resembles Freud's idea that the ego is an extension of, and outgrowth of, the id. The goal is a transformation of the unconscious negativity through the development of a strong and resilient ego and its eventual surrender. When the ego self is totally identified with such strict rational decision making, our ego's self-will, our conscious self and then our death anxiety increases. It increases because our administrative faculties are felt to be the only life, not our intuitive, vital, poetic self that is connected to the lifestream. The ego is then held onto as if it were life itself. The unconscious processes are increasingly feared, not just because they are abject and negative but because of this narrow ego identity. Our deeper poetic self is seen as not-"I," therefore not identified with; and if not me, it represents non-being or death. When the feeling self and the lifestream are identified with, then death anxiety recedes and an identification with the vaster universal life force and self gains hegemony, and death becomes safer and anxiety diminishes. This state can be encouraged by many types of meditations that empty the mind and/or by concentrating on our breathing, so that life is felt as a flow and the self is given over to that which is beyond. The problem is that in this more transcendental type of meditation, the personality often leaves aspects of the self behind that are stuck in self-interest, vanity, hubris, and the desire to triumph. When the meditation is done, the already strengthened aspects of the personality that have contact with the life force and universal self are benefited, but the fragmented destructive aspects often remain the same. Sometimes this can be seen with ascetics and spiritualists who seem very composed and poised until some serious problem arises, and then they seem all too easily knocked off balance and all too human, so to speak.

Ego Omnipotence. Another way the ego can be released is by us surrendering our sense of omnipotence. By omnipotence I do not mean some far out or crazy attempt to take over the world, but rather an inner psychological belief that although we're not necessarily in charge of all that is around us we should be. We then tend to force everything to fit our will, our wants and our needs, including the desire to force others to love us, admire us or put us first. This can also be called *the need for rulership*. It is the unconscious desire to force life in all its various ways to do our bidding instead of surrendering to the realities or exigencies of life. It is a kind of forcing reality to fit our narcissistic needs, including many outrageous ones at times, like being the center of attention, always first, always best, and always loved. This way of forcing life, or reality, to fit our fantasized wishes always creates tension and a forcing of others. In some way again, it seems a matter of life and death that others do our bidding and love us without limitation. This state of pressure causes tension and anxiety, and the forcing is the opposite of letting go into the lifestream with trust and patient understanding that you can handle what life gives you. In contrast, the accepting state does not force love or generosity or admiration or anything. This state of equanimity only comes when you let others and life be without coercion.

Reversing this tendency to force life and reality to fit our fantasy can be dealt with on a daily basis. We can try to sense through meditation or introspection the ways in which we get angry or knocked off balance when others reject us or criticize us or do not do what we feel we need them desperately to do to calm our self-doubts, such as telling us how good we are or how much they love us or simply making our life easier. When reality goes against our omnipotent self-will and we become angry, the trick is to breathe into it, acknowledge it and, after you have felt the pain of not getting what you want, see if you can tolerate the pain for a moment. If you can tolerate it for a moment, you can someday tolerate it for longer times, and then tolerance and surrender to life grows. Growth requires a sense of looking for the pain when your self-will is denied and tolerating this pain.

The childlike omnipotent state has within it a sense that now is all there is, that it will last forever and that your feelings will not change. It does not recognize that ten minutes after you receive a hurt or injury, you may forget all about it. The omnipotent child does not recognize time as temporary.

Let me also say that one of the best ways we can deal with this childlike sense of omnipotence and again surrender to the river of life is to deal with omnipotence as transference in a psychotherapy setting. If the therapist can recognize this forcing, this trying to make life fit under the domination of the patient's ego identity and self-will, he or she can help the client develop patience and also recognize how often the client demands the therapist do his bidding or bend to his will. I do not mean that the client necessarily knows that he is doing this, but it can be seen by noticing the client's undue sensitivity to any slights on the therapist's part or overreactions to any injury, such as the therapist being slightly late or distracted at moments. This needs to be kindly pointed out over time to free the patient from his unawareness. To the extent this conflict is not brought out and resolved, it will keep the client from accepting life and letting go of demands. If not resolved eventually, more pernicious emotions will accrue from the frustration of this forcing omnipotence, such as hate or a powerful desire to triumph.

Pushing for omnipotence is also a state that keeps one from loving and causes much guilt and shame, which creates a vicious circle. If you are guilty and ashamed for not being able to love, then you want more reassurance of your value from others, so you again push and force more. This is simply incompatible with a state of love. To really love in a mature way, in an ecstatic way, we have to surrender the forcing and trying to fit others and their emotions into our fantasy of what we want them to be. Any other way is really coercion and will not get us out of our bondage.

False Self. The false self is a concept originally developed by D.W. Winnicott (1965a, 1965b) that is widely referred to in psychoanalytic literature. The false self always employs the mask it feels is most useful to ingratiate itself to others. The false self shrouds the lower self and the core. The lower self has to be shrouded because if one acts on the more base impulses of the lower self it brings censure, retribution, criticism and rejection from those we care about. The lower self impulses become sublimated, reaction formatted, dissociated or repressed, and a mask of the core is presented to the world. This false self is intended to gain the greatest amount of concern, esteem, love and safety it can get, given it has base impulses that threaten its sense of well-being. The false self is developed early in life due to parental injunctions, demands and the iron template we sometimes place around our children as we value the appearance of goodness in them more than their inner subjective experience of themselves.   Robert Stolorow describes the development of a defensive self-idealization, which resembles the false self:

> From recurring experiences of malattunement, the child acquires the unconscious conviction that unmet developmental yearnings and reactive painful feeling states are manifestations of a loathsome defect or of an inherent inner badness. A defensive self-idealization is often established, representing a self-image purified of the offending affect states that were perceived to be unwelcome or damaging to caregivers. Living up to this affectively purified ideal becomes a central requirement for maintaining harmonious ties to others and for upholding self-esteem. (2013, p. 386)

The false self is designed to be a good reader of what the environment suggests is the most acceptable or glorified way of being or behaving. It is reactive in that it forsakes its own spontaneous impulses, needs and affect in favor of what it thinks it is supposed to feel, need and want. It, therefore, lacks both zest and spontaneity. How can one feel much zest for life while forsaking its own spontaneous subjectivity? The darkness in the personality that the false self is meant to hide often contains much of the zest for life. The zest for the darkness can never be liberated until the mask of the false self is deconstructed.

A cautionary note is in order here in regard to practice as a psychotherapist or in application to oneself: The core self ideal should never be used as a club. The false self, the ego and the lower self need to be embraced, accepted and integrated into the core self. The defensive and conflicted areas of the personality should never be moralized with or relegated to an abject status. Paradoxically, the more these false and lower elements are embraced as a transitional phenomenon, as in a playscape, the more they can be transformed. However, transformation needs a great deal of patience in being with the lower or negative to emerge as a different animal. If you push or moralize with or against the lower elements, they will simply be repressed and again go underground. Patience and faith in the depth analytic attitude, negative capability, and negative containment will provide the groundwork for the garden of transformation to grow. "You can never become what you want to be until you accept who you are," is an important bit of applicable wisdom from an unknown sage.

The Development of Character Faults
as a Form of Lower Self Unconscious Negativity

> *The lower self does not want anyone to receive anything from anybody else, and if it is aware of someone receiving a special boon, it seeks to destroy it.*
>
> *~ Rumi*

Since the transformation of our negative feelings, defenses and character faults, along with negative will, involves much of the low self and is a major focus of transformation in the liberation of our core selves, I think it is important to explore some of these major negative elements in some detail. When children are injured due to abuse, neglect, simple misunderstanding, or normal vicissitudes of development, they do not just feel sad or hurt and say, "Oh boy, ouch" and then move on. Hurts cause pain and anger. This anger does not just stay simple anger but typically takes the form of what we call faults. These faults underpin our bad feelings about ourselves as they cause unconscious guilt and make us feel undeserving of good things in life. They become more solidified in the personality as we grow older. There are many possible faults that we normally consider quite harmful to optimal personality development. They account for a large part of what I consider our lower selves to be.

Envy

When a child reaches out for love and feels a lack of enthusiasm, this creates pain. Enough pain and the child's longing for love turns to indifference and even hate as a defense. Hate becomes a defense because a child cannot endure rejection passively. It must, at some point, hate the rejecter and expel it from its need base to make the pain tolerable. If the child hates the rejecter, there is still a lively connection in this anti-relational way, yet the longing and pain is assuaged at least in a measure. Hate is then "love outraged."

If a child longs for a loved one who remains distant or unresponsive, the child's longing may also turn to envy. Envy contains hate in the form of wanting to spoil something about the person who is envied. The child's first object of envy, according to Melanie Klein (1975) in her work *Envy and Gratitude*, is the mother. The child longs for all that is good in the mother, and when its longing is frustrated it envies the mother for all the "goodness" she withholds and wants to spoil her so that it will not feel the pain of what is missing. This does seem to be an early childhood experience of Aesop's fable of sour grapes. The child makes the mother's "grapes" sour to salve the pain of the lack. Envy is a ubiquitous phenomenon that all human beings have—some of us very little and some to a very toxic degree. Simply put, the more envy we have, especially if we are unaware of it, the more problems we have.

Spite

Spite develops as a maneuver to have the parent or other caregiver authorities bend to the will of the child. For instance, the child may act as if it does not want love after a parent has been away or deny the parent's affection upon return. With spite, the child means to express, "If you do that again, I will punish you with my pain. Do you see how much I am suffering? I don't want you. Go away."

Contempt

Contempt forms as a method of elevating ourselves when we feel badly about ourselves. If we have received a lot of rejection or disinterest, we may conclude that if we have contempt for some others or some particular group (which we find in prejudice), we may feel better about ourselves. Often, if we have a parent who is particularly contemptuous and rejecting, we may identify with that rejecting parent. We may do so because we feel that we always wanted love from our rejecting parent, so maybe if we are rejecting in turn others may desire love from us. It may also be the more common notion that it is safer to be like the rejecting parent because we join his or her team and assume this may ward off some abuse from the rejecter. Sometimes passivity is also chosen as a defense because we may feel it is safer to acquiesce and capitulate to an abuser than fight him or her.

Arrogance, Vanity and Perfectionism

Arrogance and vanity are always attempts to rise above others as a way to resolve feelings of inferiority. Perfectionism, a close cousin to egoism, is another defense that strives to resolve feelings of inferiority and self-doubt.

When other solutions fail, the default solution is to try to become perfect. We assume that if we are just perfect enough, we can rise above our pain, inadequacies and all our doubts, and our self-loathing will then be assuaged. The perfectionism strategy is bound to fail since perfection is impossible, and the standard we cannot live up to causes even more self-doubt and self-contempt. We then set all kinds of perfectionistic standards for ourselves. We have to be the best at everything. We have to be the smartest, the most successful, the most well-liked, the richest and so forth. Many of these perfectionistic standards fail because they often contradict each other. For instance, having to be the smartest and never be wrong annoys people, so if you also have to be the most well-liked and the smartest, you find yourself in a conflict. The compulsive striving to achieve can also take you away from friends and family, with long hours at work causing others who are dear to you to feel neglected

That perfectionistic standards are unrealistic and often contradictory is not the biggest problem, however; the bigger problem is they just do not work as a realistic balm for self-contempt. Being very accomplished may feel good, but it does not resolve the feeling that deep down you are unlovable because you are unloving to others. Perfectionistic striving for success that contains within it an embedded need to triumph over others makes us feel guilty about any of our accomplishments. Perfectionism causes guilt because when we accomplish something, deep down we feel we are doing it to triumph at the expense of others.

Finally, perfectionism brings moralization about ourselves and others. It actually crashes our self-esteem because we are never perfect in our moral behavior or in our achievements. We also moralize about others, judging them contemptuously, as well as ourselves, for failing to live up to this perfectionistic standard. Again, being perfectionistic and judgmental really does not help our self-esteem. Truly, only a deeply loving attitude creates a sense that we are a good person deserving of love, kindness and fulfillment.

Angry Dependency

Angry dependency can accrue from a neglectful or rejecting parental environment. When the pain is great, the child may clamor for needs to be met, both early and later in life. A person may grow up feeling that he or she must always receive gratification of needs for caring, esteem, and narcissistic valuing way beyond healthy proportions, crippling his or her own needs for independence, autonomy and self-agency.

Entitlement

A close kin to angry dependency is a sense of entitlement, which is an extension of childhood omnipotence.. When an infant or toddler incurs either neglect of its real needs or overindulgence by its parents, it may become fixated or stuck in a childish position of expecting and demanding that the world and others always be the good parent it did not have. There will be an eternal longing and demand that life and all its inhabitants make the world comfortable and easy, much as a good mother does during a child's infancy. This entitlement causes the child turned adult to be angry at life and others all the time for failing to make the world an endless processional of comfort and good fortune.

I could spend a great deal of time cataloguing defensive negativity and character faults that arise from childhood developmental issues or trauma. It is safe to say that aggression accruing from psychic injury rarely remains just aggression; it often takes the form of the character faults I have outlined. The underlying theme is always that when a natural tendency for love and closeness is thwarted in development, negative feelings and wishes arise from our love that is "outraged." Even cruelty is just the final solution to the pain of love lost. The reasoning with cruelty is that "if I can take pleasure in producing pain, it proves to me I don't need love or anything like it."

Other Important Personality Elements

Idealized Self
Karen Horney's *idealized self* has many similarities to Winnicott's false self. The idealized self is unrealistically perfectionistic and self-aggrandizing, although possibly unconsciously, an attempt to deny vulnerability, shame, anxiety, and other dysphoric feelings. In other words, it is defensive. Again, even apparent needs for self-effacement may be the result of an idealization of effacement as a distortion of the need for perfection by appearing completely non-self-serving. Other needs, such as the need to triumph, dominate or be perfect accrue from a distorted idealized self as described by Horney. None of these unhealthy needs are designed for emotional growth, physical health or healthy emotional mutuality in relationships.

Lower Self as Child Within
As you can see, many of the faults described above—such as spite, envy, angry dependency, contempt, entitlement and more—can also be seen as childish traits. In many ways our lower selves resemble and are composed of childlike attitudes and demands and uniformed, if not ignorant, belief systems. These are things we are supposed to grow out of; therefore, the lower self in many ways can be seen as a child. It is usually the wounded child, the child whose love has become outraged through trauma. Because of the pain, we develop more aggression and other dysphoric feelings and attributes than we can

metabolize. The depth psychological approach can reach this level of the personality and bring it out of hiding and into play in treatment. When these elements are courageously faced, they can be transformed over time and with hard work, and we are then able to mature out of their grasp to a great degree.

Since we all are born with childlike needs, attitudes and irrational beliefs, we all have some elemental troubles that we have to transcend or grow out of. However, if trauma or troubles are too great or the environment does not facilitate health and maturity, pain and unmetabolized aggression become immense and unmanageable for the child, often ending in character faults, troublesome feelings and needs, and sometimes severe pathology. The child within must be embraced and held in therapy by a caring and present therapist for lower self elements to emerge and become available for transformation.

Subjectivity

An understanding of psychological subjectivity is an important element in the liberation process. As children, we all have individual idiosyncratic elements to our personality. Each child has his or her own needs, wishes, wants, dreams, ideas and self-direction, which we might call psychological subjectivity. When a child's subjectivity is not embraced, honored and encouraged, the child disowns him- or herself.

If a parent expects, however subtly, the child to fit its template of what is "good" at the expense of its inner subjectivity, violence is done to the child. Parental expectations that a child should not be unhappy, should not have complaints, should not want what it wants, should idealize what the parents idealize, should adopt without question the parents' values and morality does violence to the child's subjectivity and its core self.

This is not to say that parents should not guide, encourage and even have expectations for their children. The difference here is the forceful, sometimes tyrannical, imposition of their template on the child versus understanding the child's subjectivity, not insisting the child betray him- or herself but guiding, encouraging and pointing out consequences. The subjectivity-embracing position requires that parents understand the child's dysphoria, complaints and feelings rather than punish or reject the child for having them. It does not discourage the child from having wishes and wants, but helps shape them in rhythm with a child's organic readiness to grow and develop.

Children who are discouraged from knowing themselves and valuing their inner experience turn away from themselves and begin to see value entirely based on what parents want and, by way of transference, what other figures of authority want. This causes a dis-identification with the self and identification with others to determine what is good, valuable and right in life. People who lack self-identification must run ideas, opinions and wants through others before they will move on any decision. Or, if they do move before gaining tacit approval from authority, they do so with great anxiety, waiting for the other shoe to fall.

This lack of self-identification is crippling. They are always looking for the "book" in which the truth and what is good and right is written. Sometimes it is a literal book; at other times the book is the other person's face. Permission must be sought and received or danger is perceived in movement.

Much work has to be done in treatment for people who have had their soul murdered in this way. Through therapeutic presence, empathy and validation, over time people begin to believe in themselves again. Sometimes it is necessary to challenge people's reading of you as a therapist or have them question the therapist's opinion and encourage them to take a leap and decide for themselves to embrace an opinion or point of view. They often have to be encouraged that they have a valid position on anything in a relationship. They often assume that if they think or do something, it is wrong, that if their partner or friend doubts them or does not like what they believe or want, it is automatically invalid. They have to be encouraged to pause instead of automatically capitulating, to tune into themselves and gain a felt sense of what they think is right or good and stand behind it sufficiently to communicate their position.

This very much applies to transference. When the transference occurs, it can be gently pointed out. "Here we are again. It seems very important to you that you read me. I believe in you. What do you feel and think?"

Will

Closely affiliated with the concept of self-identification is the concept of will. Fundamentally, it is the impulse to self-direct, to affect our world and create ourselves. For Otto Rank (1945), will was a preexistent force contained in nature, much like Freud's sexual instincts, that moved the human personality to separate from the mother and forge a self and a life of its own. This will always causes anxiety as its impulse to separate and individuate brings fears of loss and abandonment. For Rank, there were two polarities of existence: the desire to unite and be at one with others, especially the mother at birth, and the desire to make one's way and create one's own self and life.

Rank's will also contains a moral component that is based on empathy and concern for others by way of the attachment of birth. The original birth experience, proffered in his seminal thesis, *The Trauma of Birth* (1973), itself was considered the prototype of all trauma and the foundation for human anxiety. However, not only does the will to individuate cause fear and anxiety, it also causes guilt in the sense that as we separate we leave behind previous objects of affection and fear they will be damaged.

Our will, for Rank, is contained by our ego. It is a condensation of the preexistent universal life force that is taken up by the individual and carries us in the creative individuation process. In *Art and Artist* (1989), Rank makes the case that we are all artists in that we create ourselves and our lives and do not merely adapt. The artist does this explicitly, but we all are the artists of our lives, and when we fail to create ourselves and our lives, we develop psychological troubles.

Early in the life of an individual, will is expressed in the developing child as counter-will. This is the common "no" to the parents that two-year-olds evidence. It is their way of beginning to define themselves and forge an independent identity. This stage of development has to be handled carefully or problems occur. If children are not allowed to use their counter-will to define themselves, it can create a masochistic-dependent capitulation and lack of self-identification, as discussed above, or an identification with the aggressor in which the children wish to become as dominant and controlling of others as the parent is with them. Finally, the children's adaptation may involve both—an outer dependent capitulation with an inner subordinate controlling impulse or an outer controlling position that thinly veils dependency.

Negative Inner Will

This counter-will can eventuate to a negative inner will that seeks to resist surrender to others and the individuation impulse. This is often hidden and creates a negative, usually unconscious, impulse in the lower self. It can drive a "no" to life, accomplishment and growth in that if the negative inner will is threatened the individual believes his or her separate existence is threatened. Good feelings and successes then appear as heralds to engulfment by others and betrayal of the self.

This negative inner will may begin to form what may be thought of as an organized force in the personality that may even shrewdly mobilize to defeat love, life and growth in a distorted sense of self-preservation. Deep within us we all have at least elements of this, which contribute to self-sabotage and negativism toward what is good in life. This negative inner will is not bimodal, meaning some people have it and some people do not. Rather, it is a continuum: some of us have it a lot and lead very troubled lives, and some have it only a little and lead pretty healthy and happy lives of engagement, growth and fulfillment.

In most depth psychotherapies, this negative inner will is often unearthed, which leads to a fundamental choice for the individual. Do I want to listen to and give in to this negative inner will or attempt to counteract this impulse and choose otherwise, choose for life and health? It really is an existential choice made from our free will. Either the positive life-affirming or a negative life-denying direction can be chosen.

It is important to note that true choice regarding negative inner will can only be made when the negative inner will is fully unearthed.

Otherwise, we are just superimposing choice over the negative inner will or attempting growth by simply prohibiting symptoms. For example, a patient reached the point where he realized that he was stuck in a position of blaming life, parents or others for his plight. If he could not challenge this anger and start to unsettle or degrade it by choosing to counteract or reduce it, he would be stuck in the position of *blaming victim* for the rest of his life. This became quite clear to him, but then he stated, "I don't have the motivation to change. I can't do it. How can I do that? Tell me." My assertion was that "This is a deep choice. I cannot make it for you. It is also not just a one-time choice but a choice that needs to be made again and again in life to really change direction." His answer: "Tell me how." My response was that "there really is no answer other than putting your will behind it. Make an intention to try to see the positive results a new choice would create here and experiment with doing it. See what it brings." The patient eventually put his will behind, taking charge of his life in this way instead of holding fast to his oppositional position. Over time, positive results begat more positive results, which affirmed an ongoing decision to stop blaming and start creating his life.

Another group client of mine was stuck on a deep level with an intention to punish life by being a child and not taking a fully adult role in his life. In psychodrama during a group, he was able to really embody his decision to demand to be taken care of. In role play, he said with great conviction to an older group member, "I insist you take care of me. I mean it." The older group member began to struggle to get away as the patient hung on him and attempted to be carried. A struggle ensued, which resulted in the patient developing a profound felt sense of how strong his demand and insistence on others taking care of him were. This moment was one of his finest in therapy and sent him on his way to take care of himself and accept an adult position in life.

In both cases cited above, if a choice point had not really become clear to the patients before they made their decision to accept an adult position in life, the decisions would simply have been superimposed over their resistance to make the choice. They would have remained a house divided in which they consciously wanted to choose adulthood but unconsciously said "no" to it. Their impulse toward adulthood then would have remained sabotaged by the unconscious "no." Only by laying the conflict bare, with the negative inner will exposed, can a truly solid free choice be made. If the inner will is not exposed, the individual will retain a much more difficult struggle between his affirming "yes" and denying "no."

Making the choice point clear can be helped along by activating the negative inner will or the "no" to life in therapy. If patients can energize their "no," it often brings it to life and puts I into relief so they can gain a felt sense of it and see it in the light of day. This moves a person toward a true choice rather than a superimposed choice. For example, a patient was steeped in a dark, intractable depression. He did not want to work, did not want to get out of bed and did not want to move. His negative intention was quite evident but not really owned as his. In his mind, it was not so much a choice as it was his biological depression causing the trouble.

In group role play, I suggested he hold onto his chair for dear life and insisted that he not move while the group members try to pry him from his attachment to the chair as exemplary of non-movement and resistance. He agreed. What ensued was a sight to behold. As group members tugged on him, he held tight; the harder they tugged, the greater the intensity of his resistance. Eventually, there was a real battle going on. They fought and wrestled, and before you knew it the patient was alive and fighting with great passion. After a while, the group gave up since the patient was not going to let go, come hell or high water. This was the beginning of his movement out of serious depression. As he energized his resistance, he also felt the truth of it, along with the passion for life he experienced while aggressively holding fast to the chair. He felt the choice point with passion and aliveness and went with the positive.

When struggling with negative inner will and change, patients often ask the question, "How do I do that? How do I choose life instead of illness?" These questions always contain the assertion, albeit unconsciously, that the person does not want to do it. I say as much to patients at times: "Your 'I can't' really means you don't want to." They often respond, "But I really do want to change." I then say, "I know you do. I believe you. But you also don't want to change at the same time. Not really. You want the world to magically change, while you stay the same. I suggest that if you truly want to change, until you find that choice point between negative inner will and positive intent you need to keep bringing out the element in you that says 'no.' Your will needs to be invested in your self-search and understanding of your 'no'; then, at some point, you can make a more wholehearted choice for commitment to change."

Self-Will

Self-will, in some sense, is the opposite of Rank's preexistent will. Self-will, which becomes carried up in our personality and leads to creative fulfillment in life, not incidentally contains an ethical dimension within it. Self-will is the little will of the ego that is pitted against others and life, that has to win and has to get its way or it is seen as tragic. It has a forcing, urgent overdriven quality to it. It is pushy and compulsive.

Some elements of self-will are discussed in Horney's concept of *overdriven strings*. This is the neurotic perfectionistic push to achieve, accomplish, aspire or obtain something in a rather ruthless or compulsive manner. Self-will also pertains to everyday micro compulsions such as demanding attention, expecting life to supply you with support, provisions, empathy and so forth.

Self-will, as with any forcing element in the personality, usually causes the opposite of the wished-for gratification. If you push people to admire you, they often think you are petty. If you expect attention, people get tired of you and withdraw. If you demand that people give you support or even material things, they feel manipulated or coerced and resist your demands.

Self-will, and the sense that you lack fulfillment of your desire, will cause tragedy and create a great deal of tension in the personality. This tension can be felt bodily. The bodily tension over time creates pain, and the pain furthers a vicious circle in which you demand more care, more admiration, more compliance, more love from others to assuage your pain. As the vicious circle progresses through life, it just gets worse unless it is addressed and worked through. The self-will, when meshed with the negative inner will, represents a potent negative element that comprises much of the dynamic force of the low self in the personality.

Chapter 3
Elements of Treatment

Felt Sense

The sensing into oneself is a very important element of self-identification and self-awareness. People experience feelings viscerally, so a tuning into one's body as self-reflection can be extremely valuable. Sadness is often felt in the throat and chest. When it wells up, it seems to flood a person's face and may result in tears. Anger, at times, feels like a storm or a pressure to hit, yell, spit or bite. Joy feels uplifting. Shame and embarrassment create a sense of wanting to hide. Fear causes a desire to flee, often felt in the limbs. Of course, erotic feelings or passion are felt in the genitals but may also be felt in the stomach, rectum or mouth as well.

Encouraging people to tune into themselves, especially when they chronically disidentify with themselves, can move them into a deeper sense of self-awareness and help them get in touch with their own story. Tuning into and validating their visceral self-experience helps people know their subjectivity, affect, and needs. This felt sense, which provides information about the self and others, is also important in developing an intuitive sense of how to handle events or problems we encounter without having to check with a book, a rule or a figure of authority. It promotes self-direction.

Basic Rule

The liberation of the core is aimed at engaging the most far-reaching aspects of the self. Since Freud, what we call *free association* has always been an extremely important tool in depth psychology. Its practice employs the basic rule of psychoanalysis. For those of you who are not familiar with the basic rule, it is this: The client says everything that comes to mind, as much as possible, and tries not to edit anything out. This allows for the greatest possible breadth of unconscious material to be examined and works against hiding aspects of the personality. When we simply ask clients things like, "What would you like to work on today" or "Tell me how things are going," we are focused too pointedly on conscious material. This is often at the expense of material that emerges spontaneously through a free associative process. Freud believed that if you are not allowed to examine everything in the psyche, it becomes like the one building in the town everyone knows will not be checked and where those who want to hide will go. When the unconscious is seriously and rigorously examined, it can aid in the greatest possible transformation of depth-abject elements in the unconscious. When the examination helps lead to a surrender of our ego to our healthy involuntary processes, our lifestream and our spiritual self, depth work is then being used for spiritual transformation.

Affect

Affects or feelings are the stuff of living. When we can deeply feel, we know we are alive and vibrant. When affect is not available, we can be conscious but be very much dead in terms of our vitality. In post-traumatic states, affects are numbed and deadened in a massive way. In life, we have all sorts of trauma: e.g., partial trauma, cumulative trauma, normative trauma, massive psychic trauma. In this author's view, trauma in various degrees, such as insults and deprivation, as well as institutional affronts by supposed caregivers, creates a state of traumatic living that causes us to deaden our life force and emotions as a way to handle these injuries.

None of us has had perfect parenting, or perfect institutional life experience. Many call this normal and maybe it is, in that trauma of the cumulative and normative kind is frequent. Just because it is frequent, however, does not absolve it from being responsible for later psychological difficulties. My contention is simply that the healthier and more supportive our development, the fewer our psychological problems and the less we need to deaden ourselves, adopt neurotic defenses and even need to act out negative states and feelings such as hate, envy and the need to triumph at all costs. We all have different levels of tolerance for trauma and psychic injury, but that does not mean the person who is without resilience or who is wounded more easily than the next is bad. Injury is still at the genesis of the psychological problem. Even the classic Oedipal complex, which many analysts have thought to be universal and normal as a genesis of neurosis, has to be questioned. If both parents are sensitive and supportive during this phase of development, much if not all of the conflict developed at this time could be alleviated. Again, strong taboos cause us to be harsh around these romantic and erotically incestuous feelings, which make it hard for both parents and children to manage the feelings without injury. No parent is perfect, and life can be far from perfect as well. Injuries are bound to accrue in our development, which cause our distortions, our life force to twist and numb, and, hence, create psychological problems.

We all use psychological defenses such as repression, denial and dissociation, but we also simply deaden ourselves to greater or lesser extents in our lives based on our histories and ability to cope. Affective numbing, in many ways, is so common it goes ignored by many psychotherapists unless it is apparent to a massive degree in post-traumatic stress disorder or depression. It goes unrecognized as one of the outcomes of traumatic living. Affects are feared as sort of screen memories that are unconscious reminders of traumatic affects and experiences. In traumatic living, any affect, including positive affects, are thought to be "heralds of the return of the repressed" as Henry Krystal (1988), one of the major trauma theorists of our time, would say. Affective memory is older than cognitive memory. Some things are never consciously remembered, but are remembered in an automatic, reflexive way by our limbic systems. When this occurs, the cognition related to the memory may be reconstructed sensitively in analysis, in rhythm with the subject's ability to tolerate affect, which helps transformation and healing occur.

Freud considered feelings as *discharge phenomena*—leftover physiological traces after instinct and thought were accomplished. This, many believe, was one of Freud's major theoretical weaknesses because it did not account for unconscious emotions such as guilt and shame, which most practitioners believe are intuitively obvious and verified by clinical work. More modern affect theory in psychoanalysis does not separate affect, thought and instinct in such a way but suggests that affect has an ideational component. Affects, when explored, can lead to great awareness of inner experience and deeper levels of our being. Affects can also be differentiated from one another and permutated into various other affects, much like water runs into different streams. For instance, hate can be a permutation of shame, shame a permutation of hurt and so on. In the end, the model or base affect is love. Even aggression is an aspect of love because it seeks to attain that which one desires. That is why all aspects of ourselves deserve love, for if we can accept all our feelings—including unflattering, painful or negative ones—they can lead us back to their source, which is love. Henry Krystal (1988) has this to say about affects:

> Just as light contains all the colors of the spectrum, so love contains all the feelings reflected in our living process. When we get a chance to observe it, as in self-healing or promoting the expansion of the conscious recognition of our selfness, we are especially prone to equate it with our life forces, or the full enjoyment of our unity and identity (p.78).

For both Henry Krystal and John Dorsey, conscious, emotional acceptance of all aspects of ourselves, including that which beforehand was considered unacceptable and unlovable, is fundamental to self-integration and self-care. They call it *conscious emotional continence*. For Dorsey and Krystal this conscious emotional containment is the pinnacle of emotional development.

Emotional Containment versus Emotional Transformation

I agree with Drs. Dorsey and Krystal's premise that conscious emotional continence is critical for emotional health and self-care, but where I diverge is that I believe this is a prerequisite for emotional transformation and health, not the final or best possible state. I suggest that negative emotions, thinking and believing can be transformed through the depth therapeutic process. Negative affects that have become part of our character will always remain somewhat painful but can be transformed over time so that they return to love more directly or be in service of love rather than against it. Conscious self-awareness and emotional continence, or being aware of negative emotions, containing them and renouncing them instead of repressing them, gives tremendous emotional relief, but it is not the final goal in my estimation. The more desired goal, which brings more enduring happiness, is living an ecstatic, loving life that goes beyond emotional continence and in a transformative direction. The more we can transform the negative, hostile, malevolent feelings within us, the happier we will be. Owning and containing these feelings is requisite, but the greater the transformation, the greater the vital liberation of pleasure and peace within us.

A bubbling, teaming, streaming core of positive feelings and a vital life force is our spiritual birthright that can be reclaimed. It is up to our individualized ego selves, in line with our core self, to practice emotional continence and self-transformation to liberate our spiritual self. When we become unencumbered by our traumatic living and deviated love, we reach our spiritual destiny.

To this end, all our abject, negative affects and negative character traits, which are typically unconscious, must be accepted into our conscious self and embraced as deviations from love, however dark they may be. There is an old Kabalistic saying, "The darker the devil the brighter the angel." I believe this is very true, and transformation of all that is negative or deviated from love within us can be a conscious goal for spiritual seekers and psychoanalysis and its offspring, depth psychology. Born out of the Kabala by Freud, it is the best tool possible to lead us back to the Kabalistic project of spiritual development.

A client named Joe was hearing critical voices that were narrating his movements throughout his house. He was also inhibited about his work, and every effort to be productive was painstakingly slow. His inhibition came from two fronts. He resented having to do anything to take care of himself in life, often thought of as a sense of entitlement, which caused a "no" to forward movement. Also, due to the projection of his own envy and hate for others who were happy and successful, he was afraid to succeed and felt it was dangerous to actually accomplish anything.

Of course, this could not be dealt with by reasoning with him that he was angry and afraid and really had nothing to fear. That approach would only engage his conscious, rational functioning and leave his unconscious "no" to movement untouched. My alternative was to engage him affectively. I coached him to go with the "no," to enliven it and bring it out. At first he seemed a little perplexed about how to enliven his feelings, so I modeled it for him. Employing something like a method acting approach, I gathered in my own experience of rage and entitlement, where the kid in me wanted everything with no cost to me. I wanted the world to be a good mother and make life ultra responsive and giving to me. In that vein, I said, "I don't want to do anything, God damn it. I want to be taken care of. God damn, give it to me, and fuck all you bastards that have nice things. I want to rip off your fucking heads and shit down your neck."

Joe smiled and laughed. There was clearly a felt sense in the room that he got it. The room seemed lighter. He said, "I should be past that, though." I retorted, in a parody of a *Saturday Night Live* psychology sketch, "You are shoulding (pronouncing it shuuting, to resemble shitting) all over yourself. None of us are ever fully past it. Some of us contain or master it more than others and transform it better, and some of us less. But it is a human sense; this demand of life to be the perfect parent is ubiquitous. Don't repress it; bring it out. Paradoxically, only by bringing it out more can you get a handle on it and begin to transform it."

I continued, "You see how easily it came to me? That is simply because I know my impish, negativistic child. You don't know yours well. You have to turn this on its head and become familiar with your imp. Get to know him. Make friends with him. Don't shuut on him." The patient laughed more. He said, "Yes, I get it." I said, "Yes, you do! I can tell you feel it." I then told him to go home and stomp around for about five minutes a day and bring out his impish, angry child.

For several sessions afterward, Joe did not report hearing any voices. I do believe this is the way out—affective tolerance and containment that breathes some air and light into the darkness, which tends to make the dark feelings less dark. As this approach is practiced instead of repression, a "yes" to life and zest for it increases, including a gradual acceptance of fulfillment.

Pathogenic Beliefs

It has already been suggested that the core self is unitive, peaceful and beyond conflict, but that life vicissitudes, hardships, trauma and constitutional vulnerabilities fracture the life force and consequent needs, desires and emotions into dualistic expression. Love can become indifference or fear. Positive aggression in service of love can become hatred, cruelty and other negative emotions. This is done, as Freud would say, by the instinct turning into its opposite as a defense. For Freud, it is easier to hate a father that is rejecting than to love him. Sometimes the hate is not obvious, as when it is repressed, and sometimes it can be turned onto the self, as in self-hatred. In this case, the self has been taken as a substitute for the father or other important rejecting figure. The father can also be replaced with someone else who can more easily be hated. This is *displacement,* and when the generalization occurs repeatedly and others are taken as hated objects, we have developed a kind of transference.

This entire cascade of dualistic expression of needs and feelings is often based on what we may call a *pathogenic belief* we learned from a psychic injury. For instance, hate, indifference or fear of a relationship may come about because a man's learned knowledge of closeness with women may be based on a childhood injury at the hands of the mother. If a mother is depressed and the young child does not understand, he may reach out for love and feel the pain of abandonment or rejection. He may then conclude all women are like this. "If I love them, I will meet with a rather dead, unloving fate, so I better avoid closeness with women." Consciously, he may long for closeness and intimacy, but unconsciously he is afraid and withdraws. He then has an unconscious conflict based on a pathogenic belief that closeness with women means pain and suffering.

Cognitive psychology has recognized the problems created by pathogenic beliefs. Authors such as Aaron Beck (1979) and Albert

Ellis (2004), are two monumental figures in this regard. A non-exhaustive list of universal pathogenic beliefs follows:

- I have to have everything go my way to be happy.
- Life is too scary to manage.
- Everyone must love me all the time or it is a tragedy.
- If I am not first, I am nothing.
- The world owes me an easy life or I have a right to punish it and others.
- Others *should* always pay attention to me.
- If someone hurts my feelings, I should punish them.
- It is important to win every time.
- I can only be happy if some external event or thing comes my way.
- My happiness depends on life being good, rich, easy, long, providing me with status, celebrity and so forth.
- I must be perfect to be loved and be happy.
- I must worry about dangerous things to prevent them from happening.
- When people don't do the "right thing," they must be punished.
- If people don't love me they should be punished.
- People are either good or bad.
- I should never have to experience, trouble, difficulty or pain.
- I am small and weak and have to have others take care of me.

The list of common pathogenic beliefs is almost endless. If we delve into idiosyncratic pathogenic beliefs, it is truly endless. Like the client with the depressed mother who developed a belief that all relationships with women would be painful and depressing, we all have individual variations of beliefs based on our unique histories. A person who is rejected when he demonstrates emotion may believe it is dangerous to feel deeply. A person who is severely criticized for touching herself may feel sexual feelings are evil. A woman whose father never demonstrates support or affection may feel all men are unapproachable.

We always need to be on the lookout for these pathogenic beliefs in our work. After they are discovered, we need to constantly challenge their veracity as they pop up and create problems for us. They are so often at the bottom of the generation or continuation of relational problems in our lives.

The Use of Needs in the Liberation Process

Maslow (1954) suggested in a more elaborate way that the focus on needs supplants biological determinism for a move to psychological growth as a fundamental paradigm. Postulating healthy versus unhealthy needs also leaves room for a dynamic interplay of non-biological, non-instinctual forces, since needs can be in conflict with other needs, rather than instincts.

Why use the terms healthy and unhealthy needs rather than ego needs and instinctual wishes? Fundamentally, instinctual wishes still bind us to an antiquated use of biological reductionism, which, I contend, is not necessary if we wish to view psychopathology as accruing from conflict rather than deficit. If we substitute unhealthy or false needs for instinctual wishes, we move the dialogue further into the psychological arena and a contextual understanding of the personality. If we exchange healthy needs for ego needs, we cover a broader, more inclusive idea of needs. After all, "ego need" is not an easy metapsychological fit with humanistic, self-psychological, intersubjective or relational theories. It also does not cover many of the developmental needs, which are important in the understanding of healthy personality development. Healthy narcissism, mirroring, attachment, positive regard and so forth are not easily included as ego needs.

Needs versus Feelings[2]

A note on how needs and feelings, known as *affect* in psychological terms, are distinguished in this paradigm. While not suggesting an exhaustive presentation of affect theory, I will address it briefly. Affect is a broad concept that connotes feelings, emotions and sometimes moods that we experience as humans. An affect is an experiential state we may or may not be aware of, that may be a precursors to a need but does not rise to the organized motivational press for discharge or gratification as does a need. If it does, it then takes the conative form of a need. An example of the difference between affect and need is that one may be angry but not have a need to punish others or oneself. A person may be frightened but may or may not have a need to seek safety. A person may feel shame but may or may not have a need to withdraw to manage shame. A person may feel love but may or may not have a need to express it. A person may feel sad but may or may not have a need to cry. Feelings, if intense, may create a need, such as a need to cry, but are phenomenologically different in that they do not press in an organized, pointed way for satisfaction, without which some sort of disorganization or disequilibrium in the personality results.

Healthy Versus Unhealthy Needs

With this situation defined, we can now ask the question, "What makes a need healthy or unhealthy?" While I will describe the differences between the two types of needs in some detail, the concepts beg for at least an attempt at a definition. My position is that a healthy need is a motivational impulse in the service of emotional growth, self-care, affect regulation and empathic appreciation of the other, without which emotional balance and health is impaired. It is clear that a healthy sense of valuing and appreciating others is part of what makes a healthy personality, and that this valuing, appreciating, and empathizing with others in good measure is a way of describing love. Hence, healthy needs are in the service of love for self and others.

---

[2] This section through the section "Needs in Harmony" (p. 87) is excerpted from "A Further Elaboration of Needs in Psychoanalysis: Needs in Conflict, Compromise and Harmony" (Sollars, 2013). Reprinted with permission from Guildford Press.

Unhealthy needs are needs that are against love and, therefore, against the *real self* and others. The real self here is analogous to Karen Horney's real self or Winnicott's true self, with capacity for concern. Unhealthy needs I define as "motivational impulses that are against or intend to do harm to our real self and others and are based on issues of vanity, power, appearances, and egoism." Unhealthy needs fit nicely into Karen Horney's position on the dichotomization of needs. We may subjectively believe that unhealthy needs are required for emotional balance and health but, ultimately, they are not; they are actually in opposition to emotional health and balance.

Karen Horney's Position on the Dichotomization of Needs

Karen Horney (1950), a student of Freud who many believe greatly influenced the humanistic psychology movement, did not use the dichotomization of healthy vs. unhealthy needs but chose to describe neurotic needs as variations of "normal needs." Horney postulated ten neurotic needs:

1. The neurotic need for affection or approval. While we all have need for affection and approval, this neurotic need morphs into a desire to please everyone at all times with little regard to other needs we may have.
2. The neurotic need for a partner. While we all desire someone to share our lives with, the need becomes neurotic when we want someone to take over our lives for us, and we abdicate our self-responsibility.
3. The neurotic need to restrict one's life to narrow borders or involutes. The counterpart of this need is the need for simplicity and decrease in the burden of our lives.
4. The neurotic need for power, omnipotence, or control. This neurotic need is overdriven and ambitious for power, with contempt for those who lack it.
5. The neurotic need to exploit others and triumph over them. The normal counterpart is the need for effectance and achievement.

6. The neurotic need for social recognition and prestige. The normal need is for some recognition and prestige. The neurotic is overdriven out of fear of becoming irrelevant and unknown.

7. The neurotic need for personal admiration. The normal need presses for some recognition and esteem from others, while the neurotic need makes one feel shamed when not the center of attention or focus.

8. The neurotic need for personal achievement. Again, the need for achievement is normal, but when neurotic it occludes other needs and the person becomes wrapped up in it at the extreme expense of self and others.

9. The neurotic need for self-sufficiency and independence. The neurotic, rather than seeking interrelationship, wants not to need anything or anyone,.

10. The neurotic need for perfection and unassailability. The desire to excel is healthy, but perfection causes one to be self-critical and unrealistic about oneself.

I would like to press Horney's dichotomization of normal versus neurotic needs even further into healthy versus unhealthy needs and suggest that the number of needs we can experience is almost limitless. Just a few of our healthy needs include the need for support, encouragement, growth, emotional development; to give and receive love, as well as to have our love received; to be creative; for ego validation, approval, vitality, excitement, harmony, peace, productivity, and agency. One complicating factor is that, paradoxically, needs can be viewed as falling on a continuum. Yet at some point, a need hits a point of variance at which it becomes discretely different; hence, healthy needs may morph into unhealthy needs. This change occurs when hostility and egoism blend into otherwise healthy needs, resulting in needs that are primarily directed to defeat or be against others. Below is a non-exhaustive list of healthy needs and their possible distortion into unhealthy needs. I say "possible" because when displacement, or even substitution, is used, the varieties of possible permutations of healthy needs into unhealthy needs are virtually endless.

Healthy Psychological Needs	Unhealthy Distortions
Safety	Passivity
Mirroring	Unlimited attention
Limit setting	Controlling behavior
Soothing	Compulsive pleasure seeking
Emotional attunement	Emotional dependence
Independence	Rebelliousness
Healthy narcissism	Unhealthy narcissism
	(unremitting need for
Agency	attention)
Assertion	Control or conquest
Achievement	Dominance
Creativity	Callous object conquest
Sexual fulfillment	Negative creation (destruction)
Altruism	Wantonness
Self-esteem	Submission
	Hubris

Further Comments on Unhealthy Needs as Being against Others
While Horney postulated "being against others" as a fundamental neurotic style, I would say that all unhealthy needs have this being-against-others quality. It is a me-against-the-world perspective and, as such, can be seen as serving compulsivity, defense, vanity and hubris. Being against others or ourselves, and even Horney's other major defensive styles of "being for others" or "away from others," are ultimately unhealthy against-other defensive organizations—in short, elements of the low self.

Regarding Horney's "being for others," when the need for affection turns to submission, there is an unconscious attempt to be so good, servile, or ingratiating that others will be seduced into giving you the affection you need. Being for others then becomes seduction and manipulation. When the need for power is used against others to triumph and conquer instead of enhance and help, it is unhealthy. The unhealthy need for withdrawal and isolation is also "against others" in that it expresses a feeling of "I want to be above you and not bother with you. I don't want to enter a relationship and deal with mutual needs and fears."

Many unhealthy needs are also nicely conceptualized as derivative of what Karen Horney (1950) describes as the discrepancy between our real and our ideal selves. For Horney, the real self is considered to be who we really are. The ideal self can be a model of who we can become that is presented to our real self. But if the ideal self becomes too perfectionistic and the discrepancy between the real and the ideal is too great, the real self becomes the despised self with an endless search for glory and an enslavement to what Horney calls *tyranny of the shoulds*. The real self then falls into the trap of Horney's defensive structures. It aims to "be against others" by "being away from others" and "above others."

In this form, the ideal self is unrealistically perfectionistic and self-aggrandizing, although possibly unconsciously, in an attempt to deny vulnerability, shame, anxiety, and other dysphoric feelings. In other words, it is defensive. Again, even apparent needs for self-effacement may be the result of an idealization of effacement, a distortion of the need for perfection by appearing completely non-self-serving. Other needs—such as the need to triumph, dominate, be perfect—accrue from a distorted idealized self, as described by Horney. None of these unhealthy needs are helpful for emotional growth, physical health, or healthy emotional mutuality in relationships.

Unhealthy Needs as Being Out of Time

Harry Stack Sullivan (1953), America's most influential interpersonal theorist, spoke of *epochs for needs*. A personal epoch is an important period of distinctive development in an individual's life that has a marked beginning and end and leads to a later, more mature period of development. Sullivan believed we are motivated by needs, which could be broken down into two broad categories. He suggested we have needs for security and needs for satisfaction. The relative balance of these two needs determines emotional health or its lack. Both sets of needs operate in the emotional field that exists between self and others. Needs for satisfaction include needs for food, warmth, shelter, oxygen, and so forth that pertain to the survival of the organism. However, there are other needs for satisfaction that relate to emotional contact and developmental epochs of the individual. These epochs are, in turn, related to psychological growth and complexity that evolve as we progress emotionally. These developmental epochs, Sullivan suggests, frame the notion that healthy needs that are "out of time" can also become unhealthy. An infant's need to experience a sense of subjective omnipotence (Winnicott, 1965b) is healthy, at that time. Subjective omnipotence is an emotional expectation and demand that life treat us as if we are special and make everything nice, easy and smooth for us, accompanied by anger when our omnipotent will is not obeyed. If there is trauma, often due to emotional neglect, during the period of time when this is a normal expectation of a child, usually during infancy, and the need carries over into adulthood, it is unhealthy. As adults, to expect the world to grant our omnipotence causes innumerable problems.

Heinz Kohut (1971, 1977) amplified the developmental progression of needs from self-object and mirroring needs to twinship and idealizing needs in the development of a cohesive self. As with Winnicott's subjective omnipotence, Kohut understood that as children we have narcissistic needs that are appropriate. An infant needs to be the apple of the parent's eye. At times, the infant needs to have the experience that the parent functions as an extension of him- or herself, much like our arms respond to our command to move. Without these narcissistic gratifications, the child is injured. At a later time, these narcissistic needs give way in intensity, and an individual gains the ability to self-regulate these needs so that gratification from external sources diminishes. As Banai, Mikulincer, and Shave (2005) state:

> With satisfaction of selfobject needs, a person's feelings of healthy grandiosity, idealization, and connectedness are strengthened, and he or she gradually acquires self-regulatory capacities. Specifically, the person can internally regulate self-

esteem and ambitions instead of requiring admiration from others. The person can develop his or her own system of ideals and goals and maintain a direction in life instead of needing to identify with a powerful other. As a result, the person becomes less dependent on external sources of self-regulation and can relate to others without demanding that they fulfill selfobject functions (p. 228).

Even though a certain amount of narcissism remains, which we may term *healthy narcissism*, if pathological narcissism does not morph into healthy narcissism as life progresses, the individual suffers. The historic life span developmental approach to needs in psychoanalysis was described by Erickson (1982) in his progression of human development, from the need for basic trust to the need for self-integrity versus despair. Each and every failure to accomplish a developmental task results in a carry-over into the next epoch of unmet needs, which makes subsequent progression problematic.

When the healthy needs of childhood are frustrated or unfulfilled, they not only carry over into later epochs but may also become distorted into unhealthy needs. For example, if the pain of a depriving or uncaring maternal caregiver is repressed, the pain may result in anger, demandingness and even the need for revenge meted out against current objects, including a therapist in the transference. Thus, a healthy need for love and empathy as a child may transform into a need for cruelty or punishment as an adult. This entire complex of healthy needs distorting into unhealthy needs can only be unraveled when the pain of the unmet needs of the past are understood and mourned, usually with the aid of reenactment in a transference dyad.

Displaced Needs

Displaced needs also lead to an overdriven intensity that can become compulsive and problematic. A need for love can become a displaced need for approval or achievement. While a measure of approval and achievement is healthy, when we lose track that we have displaced a healthy need for love into achievement, the need for achievement becomes blind and compulsive. The compulsion sets in because the *real* need is never gratified. If one is driven toward achievement to make up for a need to be loved that is repressed from childhood, one will always feel fobbed off and ungratified, despite having achieved great things. Achievement will never quite hit the spot because it does not fix the original hurt or gratify the specific need that was repressed.

To provide a more elaborate example: We can imagine a child reaching out for love and experiencing a depressed parent. Depressed parents are usually in so much emotional pain that it is hard for them to be appropriately emotionally responsive to their children. They often do not recognize their children's needs, and even when they do sometimes they do not feel enough passion to respond. If this happens enough, the child may begin to feel this natural need to be loved is frightening because its need is always being ignored. He may then conclude, usually unconsciously, that to repress this need is safer than the pain of feeling it and reaching out. Of course, repression does not mean the need has vanished. It still operates and, while repressed, it may return with all the more unconscious voraciousness, even though the open longing for love is foreclosed. The child may then become demanding of any type of attention as a replacement for love. I do not mean that it is not healthy to feel needs or desire strongly. One may be passionate about one's love for another or have a strong need to be generous. It is when one is too "attached" because of defensiveness and so desperate that an imaginary sense of catastrophe occurs when a need is not gratified that we may call it compulsive or unhealthy.

Substituted Needs

Using the same example of the child who has become compulsive about achievement as a substitute for love, as a different solution to the hurt of living with a depressed mother the child may turn the need for love into its opposite direction—a need to withdraw and become indifferent. The need for love may further warp into an opposite form. When indifference does not work in defending against the pain of needing love, sometimes hate is substituted as a way to fortify the rejection and denial of the need to be loved. As a further consequence of the substitute of hate for love, a need to punish others may develop.

In this one example of the complexity of the vicissitudes of needs, you can see there is displacement of needs and many unhealthy needs that substitute for the healthy need for love. Prime examples are the need for withdrawal to create safety, and even a need to express hate and punish others to defend against the longing for love.

Needs in Conflict

Usually when we speak of conflict, we are referring to instincts in the form of wish and defense. Abraham Maslow (1954,), one of the founding fathers of humanistic psychology, was perhaps the first noted psychologist to speak of the conflict between various needs Rather than refer to instincts, he spoke implicitly of the conflict between *deficiency needs* and *growth needs*. For Maslow, unmet deficiency needs, such as the need for safety, occluded the awareness and acceptance of growth needs such as self-actualization, union, altruism and aesthetics. From the position I am proposing, even higher order needs such as self-actualization and the need for closeness in relationships, for example, could be in conflict within the personality.

A few brief examples of this conflict include the following: a need for assertion, may conflict with a need for harmony; a need for independence may conflict with a dependent need for love; a need for achievement may clash with an unconscious need to ingratiate oneself for approval; a need for pleasure and fulfillment may clash with an unconscious need for punishment.

Here is a more elaborate example of needs in conflict: A woman may feel that she needs to assert her right for independence of thought from her husband but may realize this could cause discontent and retaliation from her husband, thus conflicting with her need for harmony or peace. A less conscious conflict of a similar sort may be a housewife who is not aware of a need for independence, represses it and consciously believes she should always be obedient. This need for independence may have been repressed due to childhood experiences in which she was persecuted or rejected for asserting her independence. Thus, she may also become unconsciously angry and revengeful toward others when her repressed need for independence causes unhealthy demands that are further spurned by partners, family and friends.

Needs in Compromise Formation

Compromise formation is another Freudian concept of great utility that has been eschewed by many post-Freudian analysts. In compromise formation, late Freudian style, the instincts of aggression and sexuality may come into conflict, resulting in a state of partial gratification of each instinct or wish and partial non- gratification or unfulfillment. By way of example, a strong aggressive instinct or desire to hurt a love object may conflict with the desire for love and sexuality, resulting in expressing a mixture of both, as in sado-masochistic erotic fulfillment. In sado-masochistic love, the individual discharges the need to hurt and the need to receive love and develops a "compromise" in that each gets a measure of fulfillment in the same event. Many later psychoanalytic theorists rejected the notion of compromise formation because it contained a reduction of all psychological problems to the biological instincts. This, they felt, was untenable, as it appeared to brace against a more humanistic, or perhaps complex, understanding of human nature. Rejecting instincts meant rejecting compromise formation.

From this position, I move away from the reduction of our psychology to instincts while not throwing the baby out with the bath water. The position I take is that, while instincts and wishes may cause conflict and compromise, needs may result in compromise formations of their own. For example, a need for sexual self-expression may conflict with a need for security in a monogamous relationship, resulting in a compromise of sexually promiscuous fantasy gratification of the need, as in fantasizing about others while making love to one's partner. A healthier compromise may be sexual fantasy and adventure shared in the same monogamous relationship. One may also compromise a need for achievement with a need for affiliation, or a need for emotional growth with the need for economic solvency (perhaps exemplified by a choice of once-a-week therapy versus five-times-a-week analysis). The list of needs in compromise is endless and only requires the use of one's imagination to develop it.

Needs in Harmony

Optimally, needs are in harmony. A need for financial remuneration may coincide and harmonize with a need for educational advancement as one becomes an educator. A need to receive love may harmonize with a need to give love in a mutually fulfilling relationship. A need for peace may harmonize with assertiveness, and a balance may develop so that one may attain a positive, healthy aggression. A need to express aggression and cooperation may harmonize in the expression of healthy competition and beget a good sport experience. A need for educational advancement may harmonize with a need for creative expression in the form of enrollment in art school. Again, the list is practically infinite, but when needs are in harmony in the personality, there is less conflict and greater peace. Recognizing unconscious needs, needs in conflict, and needs that are compromised (although freed from a biological reduction), much like previous instinctual conflict theory, results in a complex and dynamic picture of the human personality. Conflict between needs may then be interpreted, along with the fear of experiencing one's need.

Of course, this brings up the question of how we adaptively handle needs that remain in conflict while we do our work of transformation. This requires work of the ego to contain unhealthy needs, so that they do the least amount of damage to our overall personality while we continue the work of transformation. Management and containment of unhealthy needs is not the ultimate goal of the work but rather an intermediate goal on the way to increasingly better compromise formations, which ultimately lead to balance, integration and harmony of needs in the personality. This is a spiritual advancement on the way to unitive consciousness.

Of course, needs may exist in interpersonal conflict, briefly mentioned earlier, as in the case of a patient's need for an affordable fee so that he or she can pay for therapy versus a therapist's need for a good standard of living. A need for a patient to receive extra time and support from a therapist when she or he has little time available is another example. Needs in interpersonal and environmental conflict have received more play in the literature (see Rogers 1961; Maslow 1954, 1968; Ghent, 2002; Mitchell, 1991; Aron, 1996; Casement, 1982) than needs in intrapsychic conflict, which I focus on in this paper.

Case Examples of Needs in Conflict

A middle-aged patient, never married, comes into the office for premarital therapy. He has begun to get cold feet now that the wedding is within months of being consummated. Not surprisingly, his cold feet have happened before and have led to the demise of his relationships. He feels his fiancé is not erotic enough for him, but otherwise she is just "perfect." He does not know why he has lost some of his attraction and why he may want to back out, other than the nagging feeling that he doesn't feel as attracted to her as he used to be.

As he talks about her over the course of several sessions, two things become clear to me. The first is that she is far from perfect and is, unconsciously, quite demanding of him. Consciously, he feels she has every right to her demands, categorically agrees with her complaints, and feels himself to be failing her at every turn. The second thing that is clear is that he unconsciously does not feel she is perfect at all and is very angry with her but does not know it.

As the therapy progressed, several unconscious elements emerged: one was his desire to punish her by withdrawing; a second was his desire to deny the reality of her imperfection to protect her image as the perfect woman; a third was his passivity and a profound, repressed need for self-assertion; and finally, he had a strong need to please others all the time and see himself as the idealized "nice guy."

We worked with these needs from many directions. We examined his idealization of his self- image as "the nice guy" and how he erroneously believed this would ensure peace and well-being at all times. He realized it could not. If he stuffed his anger down to fit the image of the "nice guy," his anger did not really go away but went underground and showed up as a passive rejection or withdrawal from his partner. He realized this complex also contained a strong need to never be hurt and never receive anger from anyone. We worked for many sessions on how approaching life in that manner had led to a paralysis of his creative abilities, passive aggression, and troubles in his personal and professional life.

Finally, we worked on his repressed healthy need for positive self-assertion. When his fiancé complained that he was not providing her with enough money, compliments, or devotion, if he felt she was right, he would comply with her demands. However, if he felt she was being overly demanding, he began to assert himself and challenge her. He also began to ask for more privacy and time with his male friends as well. In the end, the challenges he made helped his fiancé realize that he had a subjective sense of self and his own needs. This helped her with self-reflectivity and awareness that she also was part of their relationship problems. Like ripples from a stone tossed in the water, this led to some minor changes in the fiancé, which helped him to not be so angry. His self-assertion also left him feeling he could more easily take care of himself in the relationship, so he did not need to withdraw from her to feel safe. Over the course of months, he was able to accomplish his marriage. After the wedding, he stayed in therapy for about a year to shore up some of the gains he had made and help ensure a happy adjustment to marriage. This is a rather straightforward example of the importance of understanding unconscious needs and working with them to enable their expression.

At times patients need some gratification of their needs in order to manage their intolerable affects, and the therapist's needs may also come into play in the treatment. A patient in her fifties, who was dissociative and addicted to self-vampirism, was referred to me. She loved to chew on herself or cut herself to allow the blood to flow, which she then sucked up and drank with passion. She told me this afforded her great relief from an inner anxiety and tension. As therapy moved on, it became clear that she had a strong need for quasi "rulership" of me in the therapeutic hour, as well as a more obvious need for self-punishment. She did not want me to have any other patients, she wanted my office decorated in certain ways, did not want me to drink coffee during our session, and so forth. I actually spent years gratifying many of her needs to adjust pictures, rearrange furniture, and adjust sounds in my waiting room, such as a sound-screen noise. This seemed to actually be necessary for her to tolerate the therapeutic frame. When I was not responsive in this way, she would become more dissociative and develop conversion reactions of fainting, falling, and stereotyped involuntary movements. As time passed and the therapeutic alliance took greater hold, she began to decrease her need for these adjustments to maintain affect regulation. It seemed as if I functioned as a good self-object for a long time. I made interpretations of how my involvement in this way was something she had lacked early in her development. I do think that if I had not gratified her needs early on in this way she would not have even been able to tolerate the therapy and would have broken it off.

Functioning as a self-object in this way, not just with empathy but responsiveness to her actual need for domination or "rulership," required that I give up some of my own needs. My need to keep a tight frame and my allegiance to my previous theoretical position of non-gratification of patients' needs also had to be altered. I believe this challenged my need for a consistent professional identity, which in the end had to be subordinated to a greater need—to really help my patient when she was in such pain.

Interestingly, all these ferocious demands and needs were isolated from her angry feelings when she came into session. She simply wanted these things but was not aware of anger accruing from their frustration. One day she became angry because she heard a distant sound coming from somewhere in the building, a sound I could not prevent or adjust. Sometimes she screamed and yelled during session but would never own that she was angry. This time she began to pull at her cuticle to draw blood, saying, "I have already begun to work on this spot and I can get blood from it pretty easy." As she began to tear at herself and blood emerged, I said, "I think you are at least a little annoyed with me because you feel I should protect you from the invasion of these noises into our sanctum here. When I can't, it hurts and the anger comes. You feel you can't tell me because I might get mean and let more noises come. I think you want to bite me and draw my blood so you can have me inside to protect you, as well as punish me for my failure. Since you really can't bite me, you bite yourself."

This seemed to relax her, even though she would not be denied the pleasure of drinking that bit of her blood.

These types of interventions, after a period of gratifying her self-object and "rulership" needs, over time helped her feel she could talk about her aggression, which along with her unconscious guilt for all this aggression was the main cause of her need for punishment. Eventually, she could also discuss her unrealistic angry/dependent need for me to protect her against any failure in her environment. It also led her to mourn the lack of appropriate protection and support she experienced due to various childhood traumas. She began to feel that her childhood need for omnipotence and "rulership" could not and need not be fulfilled now. Where once she needed soothing and protection from invasive elements, she realized the therapist could not do that for her now and that she needed to develop her own frustration tolerance. Eventually her need for self-vampirism became much less urgent and took the form of a compromise of mostly token self-biting that seems rather common to most people who bite their nails.

Prometheus Bound: Breaking the Chains
of Unconscious Guilt and Low Self-Esteem

Many of us clinicians, especially as we have advanced past the beginning stages of becoming a psychotherapist, have struggled with clients who seem to be addictively stuck in negative situations. Clients will stay hopelessly lost in an abusive relationship. Women may be verbally or physically abused but like the moth to a flame return to the abuse again and again. Men are more often taken advantage of while they passively complain about being exploited. Other clients seem hopelessly stuck in an attitude of never feeling adequate in any endeavor in life. Every positive movement they make is met with a backward pull. We provide encouragement and support. and they take one step forward and then one step back.

Many people feel that they are just not comfortable in positive situations. They should be somewhere else. They sometimes are unable to experience the pleasure of even very wonderful events.

These people unconsciously avoid pleasure in life even while they consciously long for it. This avoidance of pleasure we label *anhedonia*.

Our fears of success, advancement, fulfillment, acceptance of pleasure and abundance have all been conceptualized and addressed in various manners. Freud's Oedipal complex, castration anxiety and unconscious guilt present one important paradigm. Cognitive behavioral schools of psychology have developed treatments that have addressed fears of success with the use of reinforcement schedules, the reshaping of erroneous beliefs, and affect regulation. Mindfulness techniques and various forms of meditation imported from spiritual disciplines have also been employed. Object relations theorists have posited the attachment to negative, introjected parents as causal in the development of the inhibition of varieties of positive experience. Self-help "gurus" have encouraged the use of affirmations and positive self-talk. All of these schools and techniques have merit and have been of enough help so that many find relief from their inhibitions to fulfillment. Others, though, have only had partial success with these schools and techniques, while still others perhaps have been helped very little.

My fundamental assertion regarding specifics of the work I am suggesting is that where unhappiness and lack of fulfillment, pleasure and joy exist after repeated attempts to grab the brass ring, you can bet there is an unconscious inhibition or "no" to the fulfillment. You can also bet that the inhibition or "no" to fulfillment is based on unconscious guilt that makes us feel unworthy of the fulfillment we seek, even if we consciously think it should be ours. The reason for lack of fulfillment is not outer circumstances, people standing in our way or fate as much as it is the deeper part of us that says "no" to what we long for. We are our own worst enemy in this regard. This text is an attempt to help liberate our clients from this position and help them find their way to fulfillment and liberation by uncovering and dissolving their unconscious guilt.

I will give a brief example of how pernicious our desire to defeat ourselves can be. Years ago I had a woman client who was chronically underemployed but was finally working toward a promotion. On the way to an important meeting to enhance her promotion abilities, she stopped at a gas station to fill up. The first problem was that she locked her keys in the car. The other problem was that she left the car running. And the final problem was that she left the car in gear. The car began to move as she helplessly watched. It picked up speed as it moved away and eventually crashed into a building. She came to the session in tears and confessed that in some way she knew she had sabotaged herself as she had always done.

The Nature of Unconscious Guilt

Sigmund Freud (1924) struggled with unconscious guilt as an inhibiting force to fulfillment and emotional health. He described it in this way: "In analytic treatment we come across patients to whom, owing to their behavior toward its therapeutic influence we are obliged to ascribe an 'unconscious sense of guilt'" (p. 166). He went on further to propose that this unconscious sense of guilt can create a "need for punishment." After working with many patients, he found another interesting factor. He discovered that many of those he treated could replace one symptom for another, and when one symptom would be present the other symptom or problem would go away. He then proposed that the deeper motivating force was a need to not be well, and even conversely, to suffer. Freud went on to put it thusly:

> It is instructive, too, to find contrary to all theory and expectation, that a neurosis which has defied every therapeutic effort may vanish if the subject becomes involved in the misery of an unhappy marriage, or loses all his money, or develops a dangerous organic disease. In such instances one form of suffering has been replaced by another; and we see that all that mattered was that it should be possible to maintain a certain amount of suffering (p. 161).

Freud believed the reason that we feel this unconscious sense of guilt is because we have internalized our parents', and by extension our community's, values and rules and developed what we call a superego or conscience. Furthermore, what happens in our unconscious may be more powerful than our internalized rules. Thus, even though we behave according to our rules, such as sharing with our friends or acting nicely toward our neighbors, our unconscious may contradict our conscious intention and behavior. In our unconscious, we may not want to share at all and believe that "to share is to lose."

For Freud, the bigger problem regarding inhibition of unconscious guilt was his belief that there is an irrational, unconscious equation between thoughts and actions. That is, if we think it unconsciously we have already "done the deed." Therefore, if we are mad enough at a neighbor to punch him, we unconsciously believe we have punched him in the nose. Following the belief that we have punched the neighbor in the nose because we unconsciously wished it, unconscious guilt arises. This is a major reason Freud thought it was so important to help the unconscious become conscious. "Where id was ego shall be" is his famous statement. The ego is the agency of our mind that can reason with the irrationality of our unconscious.

I differ in one important way with Freud's notion that unconscious guilt is often the ball and chain that keeps us from achieving fulfillment and happiness in our lives, and that not addressing unconscious guilt often renders psychotherapy ineffective. I think the equation in our unconscious that our thoughts equal actions is not the most important factor. My position is that if we automatically feel badly about ourselves and feel undeserving of good things in life to the extent that we are negative in our unconscious, we feel unloving. It is the actual feeling of spite, resentment, envy or hubris that takes its toll. If we walk around feeling unconsciously bitter and resentful, or wish to defeat others deep down (often with outer appearance to the contrary), we just do not like ourselves very much and our self-esteem crashes. This low self-esteem and self-disliking wreaks havoc on our personality and our lives.

To go further with how my position differs somewhat from Freud's, whereas Freud places an emphasis on the superego or conscience as being an internalization of parental and cultural standards, I believe that deep within us we have an exacting mechanism in our core that is automatic: *When we are against our brothers and sisters in life, however conscious or unconscious, we just feel badly about ourselves.* Winnicott's (1965b) capacity for concern and St. Paul's adage "The law is written on the heart" attest to this deeper inner sense of morality.

This automatic moral reflex stems from our core self, which knows when we are unloving regardless of internalized rules and standards. In fact, at times this reflex may be different than worldly standards we live with. For example, when Rosa Parks said to heck with this law about sitting on the back of the bus, she went against outer law and aligned with her inner law of justice. When Martin Luther tacked his edict on the door suggesting you cannot buy your way out of misdeeds, he challenged outer law and embraced inner law. These are major historical examples. Every day, however, we have examples of little moments we may be able to "get away with" but feel badly about. Leaving a party early and not helping to clean up, criticizing our children, withholding affection or positive thoughts from loved ones, being resentful of a friend's accomplishments are such examples.

I am not suggesting we are perfect and that anyone should now keep a watchful eye out for these "transgressions." I believe that would lead to moralization and repression, which only drive unconscious negativity underground where it continues to do its damage to our self-esteem. I actually suggest the opposite, which is that we look for and pay attention to our negativity and bring it out to our conscious awareness rather than repress it. When we become more aware of our competitiveness and spite or envy, for example, we begin to get some psychic distance from these feelings and have a sense of humor about them so that they begin to slowly dissolve over time. When we register the pain of wanting ill for our neighbor, wife, child, or friend, for example, and contain this feeling by virtue of noticing the consequences and bad feelings this creates, we automatically begin to feel we do not want to keep doing or feeling the things we are feeling. It is this conscious containment, psychic distance and perspective that begins to release us from our attachment to these negative feelings and thoughts. Sometimes, then, we may laugh at how silly we are or grieve the fact that we feel and harbor such negative thoughts and feelings. In both cases, conscious awareness and containment of the negative is critical rather than doing our customary repressing and pretending to ourselves that we do not harbor such feelings.

We automatically feel badly because we have an exacting mechanism in us that is morally compassed, known as our core self, which registers any unconscious negativity and leads us to feel undeserving and badly about ourselves. This core self is the deepest element of our being and is inherently grounded in morality and, at times, transcends outer rules, laws and standards. This core self grows inexorably toward the good like a plant grows toward the light, if given enough support and help. Of course, we face so many pratfalls, traumas, institutional suppression of our real needs, neglect and such that no one escapes childhood without injury and, therefore, the development of unconscious negativity is rather universal.

The Marriage of Pleasure and Pain

We all have a certain amount of negativity and destructiveness, as well as a certain amount self-defeating behavior, self-sabotage and self-loathing that stems from our negativity. A powerful reason that negative feelings and self-defeating behavior cannot be given up is the little-understood fact that pleasure often gets mixed with our destructiveness early in our development. We all have had experiences in childhood where a certain suffering took place. The pain could be an overall rejection by a constant critical and disparaging attitude that is directed at us. The pain could be the result of indifference by a parent. It can even come from witnessing the abuse or degrading of others. If you meditate about it, you may remember that a certain insidious process may have taken place at some point when you experienced your pain. That insidious process is the marriage of pleasure and pain. In order to make the suffering, embarrassment, neglect, shame and so forth more tolerable as a child, you began to cope with it by taking some enjoyment in your suffering. It may have taken the form of self-pity—"Woe is me. Aren't I nobler for suffering thusly?"—or just taking a subtle pleasure in the pain. This was always an attempt to adapt, to cope with the pain and make it less intense. The trouble is that it begins the marriage of pleasure and pain.

This marriage causes a mingling of pleasure with the pain of our self-destructiveness and, after the wedding takes place and a habit develops, it makes giving up negative feelings and self-defeating behavior very difficult. With this attachment, we start to feel that if we are not involved in some negative drama, feud or long-suffering situation we lose a sense of zest and vitality. It feels like we are giving up feeling alive to leave the negative behind. This explains why we often have such a stubborn attachment to negative gossip, drama or focusing on problems instead of feeling zestfully positive and enjoying what is good in life.

This marriage of pleasure and pain also explains some of our negative romantic attractions. Many feel that "good" people are often boring and gravitate to "bad boys" or "bad girls." When we have too much of this marriage of negativity and pleasure, we only feel alive and erotically interested if we are in a rejecting relationship with someone who is half committed or if there is a danger of losing the person. This marriage can be brought into our sexual lives as well. In such cases, sexuality becomes more exciting if there is some humiliation or domination taking place, and having joyful sex in positive relationships and positive sexual experiences becomes severely compromised. This can make a long-term relationship and marriage hard to accomplish.

When this marriage of negativity and pleasure has only a remote connection to our sexuality, it resembles what Freud (1924) called *moral masochism*. Moral masochism can be described as a need for punishment that pushes us toward suffering in life in areas other than just our romantic relationships. This could be an attachment to a job we feel is important but brings us a good deal of suffering. Working too many hours for the sake of family, tithing for a church or giving to any cause that brings us severe consequences can also fit the picture of moral masochism. Any "positive" cause can be co-opted by moral masochism and used to suffer over.

Sword of Damocles

The *Sword of Damocles*, a late classic Greek myth brought into European consciousness largely by Cicero, the Roman poet (1877), is illustrative of the constant worry of those who suffer from moral masochism. Damocles was a member of the court of the notorious King Dionysius II of Syracuse. In an effort to ingratiate himself to the king, Damocles obsequiously fawned over him and told him how wonderful he was and how wonderful the king's life was. The king offered to switch places with Damocles for a time, which Damocles speedily agreed to. However, to symbolize the life of a royal, the king strung a sword over his throne, where Damocles now sat, and hung it by one hair of a horse's tail. After a time of suffering under the constant worry of the sword falling, Damocles asked the king if he could leave his place on the throne. He realized he no longer wanted to be so fortunate as to sit on the throne.

Many of us often worry endlessly and obsessively, as if a sword is hanging over us, especially when things are going well. If things go well, we can always find something that is wrong or possibly about to go wrong that we can focus on and worry about. Worry is a form of suffering that gratifies our need for pain and punishment, but it seems so "everyday normal" that no one suspects it as an unconscious excuse for suffering.

Worry is a great compromise. If we just suffer enough over any accomplishment or happy event, then we feel we have paid the price. The worry is always a bargain to pay for the price for any happiness. Most people always feel that there is a legitimate reason to worry, and only after the worried-over event passes do they think the worry was silly. We often find the apparent " reason" for such worry. After all, "I might fail, you know." Only by stepping back do they realize that they compulsively worry. However, most people never realize the real reason why. If we have a need for punishment, "worry wartitis" fills the bill. People who worry compulsively have a very hard time giving it up and enjoying themselves. They are afraid of the free-flowing, melting quality of pleasure and happiness. All of us have this fear to some extent, but chronic worriers have it in abundance.

Prometheus Bound

Another myth used to describe our suffering is Aeschylus' myth of Prometheus. Henry Krystal (1985) uses this myth to illustrate our inability to care for ourselves and our attachment to negative events and behaviors in life. His portrayal of our inability to align with positive, pleasurable feelings is encompassed by what he terms the *Prometheus complex*. In Aeschylus' myth, Prometheus is portrayed as a Titan who stole fire from Zeus and gave it to mortals to care for themselves. Zeus then punished Prometheus by chaining him to a rock in the Caucuses, and every night an eagle would come down and peck out his liver. The liver would grow back again by day, putting Prometheus in an endless cycle of torture for his transgression. Zeus also sent Pandora in retaliation to unleash the evils, plagues and diseases that caused death for mortals, leaving only hope left locked in her jar.

The gods' fire represents our ability to care for and soothe ourselves. In broad context, it also represents the ability to create vital, positive feelings that promote health. Prometheus' crime of helping mortals care for themselves analogizes a sense we often feel: that it is dangerous to care for ourselves. Somehow, if we do reach for and enjoy "good things," we are committing a crime. The punishment in this myth is great. Not only is Prometheus chained and tortured endlessly, but Pandora's evils cause endless illness, suffering and death.

For Henry Krystal (1988), this inhibition in self-care is derived largely from parental injunctions that result from parents co-opting the child's movement toward individuation and self-care. He equates the self-caring functions to an assumption in our unconscious that this is a God-like power, which, he believes, the child learns through idealization and experience that the mother is supposed to possess. To own these abilities is prohibited and is a kind of blasphemous usurpation of power. Krystal illustrates several prototypical relationships that may result in this inhibition of self-care. The first is a mother who may overtly "punish or discourage any self gratification or autonomy by the child" (p.185). The mother in this case may be frightened that the child's independence will cause her loss and pain, so unconsciously she will undermine this movement. She may be jealous of friends or others in the child's life and hold the child "close" or even disrupt an attachment to others or transitional objects.

Another prototype is the parent who sees the child as an extension of him- or herself and makes the child identify with his or her wishes and aspirations, co-opting the child's sense of self. This leads the child to feel that the self-caring functions are reserved for the parents, and thus these functions become psychologically walled off. Finally, a parent who somehow feels autoerotic functions are shameful will discourage self-touching, self-stimulation and even the joy of sexual curiosity as bad, thus inhibiting auto-erotic satisfaction. Sadly, in severe psychopathology, parents may even be jealous of their children and express it by punishing fulfillment.

Elsewhere in his magnum opus, Henry Krystal (1988) proposes that the "walling off" of maternal self-caring functions takes place in the face of extremely aggressive feelings toward an internalized representation of the parent. He also states that this aggression "sets the limits on kinds and numbers" of clients who can be brought to the completion of psychotherapy. I believe this aggression, much of which is unconscious, is the dark night that enters into treatment and prevents a positive result—not simply because people are frightened and ashamed of it, but because unless it is worked through and modulated considerably, the guilt from it will cause a sense that "being well" or "living well" is a crime. After all, we think, "if I am such an angry, negative, punishing person deep down, if I do well I should be punished even more." Life becomes a compromise with this complex because every forward movement or positive feeling heralds future punishment and attack, as in the case of the myth of Prometheus. The unconscious negativity is what locks in the self-destructive impulse, self-defeating behavior and resistance to fulfillment and growth. This is what makes the internalized or learned parental injunctions against self-care so intractable. Returning to Freud, it creates what resembles an id resistance or a pull in the unconscious, like an intransigent habit pattern toward the negative.

In psychotherapy, it is almost never enough to simply interpret or understand the internalized parental injunctions against self-care to find liberation from them. It is also almost never enough to gather in the transference around the capacity for self-care and anger about the parental injunctions. Although both of these therapeutic maneuvers are very important, the need for self-punishment and the inhibition toward self-esteem, self-care, growth and happiness will remain pernicious if unconscious negativity is not contained and worked through.

Prometheus' Chain

Extending the mythology of Prometheus, I would like to describe in psychological terms the chains that bind us in Promethean fashion. There are seven important links in this chain. Understanding the entire chain is important, for practitioners and clients alike, in order to achieve liberation from these chains. Some elements need to be understood and worked with extensively for liberation. I will give a brief explanation of the chain and then delve into it in more depth.

Every child has a need for love and affection, empathic caring, joyful interest, and a constant supportive presence from parents. This longing for love and its injury is the beginning of the vicious circle. Many parents fail enormously in this regard. Some parents are so wounded, so injured themselves that they cannot be present and giving of themselves emotionally to the extent a child needs. Other parents, because of their own dependency and unfulfilled desires, treat children as extensions of themselves and block out their children's subjectivity and individuality. Ultimately, however, no parent is perfect, and every child must deal with some injury and neglect. Whatever the degree of injury, abuse, neglect, lack of joyful interest a child receives is roughly proportional to the hurt, pain and anger that is provoked as a response to the parents involved. The childhood hurt is the *first element* in the Promethean chain.

The anger response to the hurt, the *love outraged*, is the *second element* in the chain. The anger, which emanates from a longing for love, is a common response by children to the abuse or neglect they have received and, at this point, is an instinctive response to try to change the situation of abuse. However, parents often just take the childhood outrage as proof the child is bad, which reaps more punishment on the child or further rejection instead of helping the child understand the anger. Rather than helping, parents often shame the child instead for the outrage.

A further effect of hurt, shame and outrage is the fixation on childhood omnipotence, which is the *third element* in the chain. All children expect and need a time in the first couple years of their life when "the road rises up to meet them"—that is, parenting very much attuned to them, parents who joyfully engage them and are available to meet their needs for mirroring, empathy and vitality. When a child is injured very early in life, he or she gets fixated in a desire for the world to be totally available and supportive to them. They then feel *entitled* to their expectation of omnipotent, positive response from the world at all times. This sets up a ubiquitous expectation of a life of entitlement and "justified" anger and blame when their childish demands are not met. Of course, this remains unconscious, and it further locks in a cycle of angry expectation, demand and blame and, thus, further outrage.

Shame and fear drive underground the anger felt for the parent for the abuse or neglect. The child feels that expressing the anger felt toward the parents that he or she loves will either bring further abuse or less love. The child then represses the feelings. Just because the feelings are repressed does not mean they are gone. They are only gone to the conscious mind. The unconscious negative feelings simply smolder underground. As they smolder, they create bad feelings about the self, thus causing low self-esteem and unconscious guilt. This low self-esteem and unconscious guilt constitute the *fourth element* in the Promethean chain.

The low self-esteem and unconscious guilt create a deep-down feeling of being undeserving of good things and even the "need" for punishment. The guilt causes a sense of deserving punishment because of unconscious "badness," and this sense of deserving punishment gives rise to a need to court the punishment. We feel that since somehow we deserve punishment, it is bound to happen so we might as well get it over with. At least ,if we get it over with by our own volition, we spare the further embarrassment of punishment at the hands of others. We sort of beat them to the punch and feel at least that "I'm on top of it, and I'm exerting some control." This is a masochistic compromise, the *fifth element* in the chain, in which we assume that we gain a measure of relief by warding off future danger by bringing on the punishment ourselves.

The *sixth element* in the chain has to do with a defense of projection. Often, this goes along with the fourth element of self-punishment or, rather, emerges when turning the aggression on ourselves fails. With projection, we deny the negative feelings and destructive attitudes in ourselves and project them onto others. This causes us to almost always believe others are mad at us, jealous of us, spiteful toward us and so forth. Any element we cannot accept in ourselves we experience as coming at us from others. We then become reinjured by others constantly because we always believe others are feeling negative, judgmental and mean toward us. This further locks in the Promethean chain.

This compulsive dependency is the *seventh element* in the chain. It chains adults to a child-like tendency to look for others to act like parents and give us constant reassurance. The compulsive dependency causes an alienation from our needs, and the dependency also brings about more anger at those we love because the compulsivity can never be really fulfilled and drives people away. This results in more rejection and worse feelings about ourselves. The chain begins to close around us, and we are now as children. We have then become so much more vulnerable to rejection, hurt and anger, which cause more pain negativity, unconscious guilt. And around it goes, accelerating our problems and furthering our need for attachment to negative life situations and avoiding fulfillment.

Breaking the Chains that Bind Us

The fundamental elements needed to break the Promethean chain are self-reflection and negative capability. Negative capability is the capacity of human beings to reject the totalizing constraints of a closed context and explore new understandings of the event or context. The sense in which I am using negative capability describes our ability to leave behind all of our narrow perspectives on ourselves, all of the attitudes that say we must be this way or that, be good at all times and so forth. It is the capacity to suspend these self-flattering perspectives and see ourselves in a new light, encompassing that in us which is also negative. A tall task, I would say, but one that should be attempted. However closely we can approach this state, it promotes our capacity to self-examine reality and overcome the negativities that are discovered. This is also a state sought after in psychotherapy. With the support of a therapist who has an attitude of acceptance for all a client brings forth—and even all that still remains hidden—the client begins to accept greater aspects of self that he or she had previously not wanted to face. It has a similarity to the ancient Greek word e*poché,* which describes a mental state in which all judgments about the world are suspended to allow for a fresh look at reality. Edmund Husserl (1970) used it in his phenomenological reduction, which is a systematic attempt to suspend judgments about an event, an experience or phenomena as it appears to consciousness. Here, I use it as a method of self-reflection in which we suspend judgments about ourselves, of how we are supposed to be, in an effort to see ourselves as we are.

This self-reflection must be applied within psychotherapy or on your own, if you are not in treatment. It needs to be applied to the various points of the Promethean chain or vicious circle in an effort to lift these points into awareness: 1) childhood hurts, which we have denied and repressed, 2) the anger and fury felt toward the parent and the hurtful experience, 3) the resulting fixation on childhood omnipotence, 4) the guilt and low self-esteem because of the outrage, 5) the "beating others to the punch" with self-punishment, 6) the paranoid projection of our negative feelings onto others, and 7) the compulsive need for others' approval and reassurance, which leaves us ripe for more hurt and anger.

It takes a long time to change the habit pattern of the negative vicious circle. These various points can be easily repressed again rather than practicing containing them more consciously through vigorous self-reflection. I will review the various points that need to be worked through more thoroughly.

Elaboration of the Promethean Chain
and Working through in Psychotherapy

Childhood Hurts

Examining problem areas in our current relationships is one good way to discover the hurt of our childhood. We can often find the echo of childhood hurts in our current problems. We all long for perfect love from our parents, who fall short in large or small measure, and because we are usually unaware of the extent of our hurt, we go about life trying to fix these hurts. This usually involves some sort of re-creation of childhood difficulties in later years. We may choose love partners that resemble both the positive aspects of our parents and the way that they injured us. This is called a *re-creation* or a *reenactment* of our childhood hurt. It is common for us to repress and deny these childhood hurts, so it is difficult for the therapist to bring these into awareness. We want to repress or forget about them because they are painful, or just pretend they never happened, which is denial.

The therapist has to examine the history of the client's childhood to ferret the hurts out with questions about the nature of the emotional relationship between the child and the parents. Were the parents able to be emotionally available to the child? Did the parents empathize with the child's hurts or subjective needs and experience? Children need this desperately. Were the parents able to allow the child's individuality to emerge? Some parents create a sort of template that the child is supposed to live up to that suffocates individual expression. Was the child able to complain or have bad moods without being criticized too harshly, feelings we consider dysphoric? While children need to be guided to be constructive and positive, if parents "force the fit" by harsh criticism and punishment rather than allowing dysphoric feelings and talking the child through them with support, the painful feelings just go underground, are repressed and are never allowed to mature.

Were parents able to enjoy their child? This is an important question. Therapists should not settle for a glib answer to this question but explore it thoroughly. Many parents are so stressed that they just do not have time to enjoy their kids. Other parents are just so angry that it spills over to the children. They are mad that life is hard, that they have to work so much, that they do not have enough money and so forth, making the child feel guilty about just existing because his or her existence puts pressure on the parents.

Conversely, some parents, such as "helicopter parents," may even over-parent in some obvious ways, giving their children everything they want. They may confuse this with love. Loving parenting requires setting boundaries that children sometimes will not like and then helping them cope with their frustration and anger, not by shaming them but through understanding. Through parent's guidance, children also need to develop tolerance for frustration and an understanding that happiness does not come by always getting our way but through acceptance that we are okay even if we do not always get our way. Over-parenting is actually an apology for the love parents have not given their children in the form of kind limit setting.

All of us as children desire unconditional love, positive regard, kind boundary setting and joyful interest in who we uniquely are. Parents are never perfect and always fall short in some measure. In some cases, children even amplify minor issues and their injuries with parents. In either case, by omission or commission, we are hurt as children. This hurt is often repressed and the injuries often rationalized or denied. Many grow up compulsively asserting how much they were loved and that they had perfect childhoods because they were loved in some measure. They grow up angry, sometimes without being conscious of the anger, unhappy and with various problems, never quite knowing why. Often because they are angry, consciously or unconsciously—and even if they blame others—they attribute their suffering to a sense that they are inherently bad.

Love Outraged

Children do not easily shrug off parental abuse and neglect. If a child is severely neglected by a depressed parent, the child may not even register it consciously because he or she does not have the words to symbolize and represent the abuse in verbal memory. The child may have what we call a *limbic* or *emotional memory*. The limbic area of the brain records the event emotionally and it is remembered emotionally. As the child grows older, he or she may feel a sense of panic when a loved one is gone for a while or is not emotionally available, and the reason is not clear. It is recorded in the emotional and not understood in our usual way. The child may then develop a fight-or-flight response when someone leaves. The fight is anger at those who are leaving or not emotionally available. The flight is fear, which, for them, is of unknown origin.

These types of problems have to be reconstructed in the therapy. By piecing together what the child, who now is a client, says about his or her early environment and working backward to reconstruct logically what path earlier, similar hurts would logically follow, words are given to lost events and memories can be filled in or, as we say, reconstructed. This reconstruction is also done with clients who employ defenses such as denial and repression. Over time, the truth of their early psychic injuries can be brought back and made clear emotionally. Whether or not the childhood hurts are reconstructed, one thing is for sure: The child, who may now be an adult, has a lot of outrage at the hurts he or she received. The child may not register them consciously, and the less conscious the worse the effects will be in the personality. However, hurts always cause the *love to be outraged,* and the child carries the weight of this anger into adulthood unless worked through. This entire complex, when not conscious, leads to unconscious guilt.

Childhood Omnipotence

Childhood omnipotence is a tricky concept to understand. It is not actually that the child is omnipotent, of course, or that the child believes that she or he is omnipotent, but rather that the child feels entitled to be omnipotent and to be ruler over others. The child expects his world and others, by way of transference, to be at his beck and call and to meet unlimited demands for love. The world should always admire, put the child first, and meet all needs and desires that the child has. And if the world and people in the world do not meet all the child's needs and desires, the world is experienced as bad. The child develops a sense that others need to be punished to get them to shape up and act right, and finally be good parents. Sometimes this omnipotence even extends to the environment, with the child demanding good weather and warm breezes, and if the environment doesn't caress the entitled one, the child within the adult becomes mad. An omnipotent child within an adult may even be mad at the rain for being wet.

This omnipotent entitlement causes a cycling of anger every day in small and large ways. If the day's work is too hard, the child within is mad. If friends need us too much and cause a burden, the child within is mad. If loved ones have expectations of mutual care and concern from us, the child within is mad. Finally, if weather is too cold, too hot, too wet, the child within is mad because the world by way of transference is failing the child again.

This, of course, is never fully conscious because we are always ashamed or embarrassed at this childish omnipotence and entitlement. We don't want others to see it, and we don't want to recognize it ourselves because it causes shame. The shame comes because somewhere in the psyche we know the demands for omnipotence are childish and unreasonable, so we hide them. In fact, a major turning point in the life of an individual's spiritual and emotional growth is the recognition and acceptance of this childhood omnipotence.

Unconscious Guilt and Low Self-Esteem
Rather than guilt from Freud's point of view, stemming almost entirely from internalized parental standards, our real guilt comes from an exacting mechanism hard wired within us called our core self. Inherently, we feel bad when we harbor antipathy and ill will toward others, even if it is in our unconscious. Because of childhood hurts we become angry and outraged toward our parents. The earlier and the greater the hurt, the more angry the child becomes. Even though the child may be repressed because of fears of retaliation for the expression of anger toward his or her parents, the anger does not go away. In fact, when the anger is repressed, it has virtually no chance of being worked through or resolved through a natural maturational process.

Often there are numerous false guilts that arise when a person has unconscious negativity. Freud noted this long ago in his lecture on the need for punishment. He noticed that the depressive person will feel guilty about all kinds of things such as others' problems, that they are burdens on others or even that they are responsible for crimes they could not possibly have committed. This acts are a displacement of their real guilt for the anger they feel toward their loved ones. To this end, it is interesting to notice how many people make false confessions when they find out about some criminal activity in their area in the newspaper or on television. This often becomes a problem for law enforcement officials.

Another naturally occurring consequence of unconscious guilt is a sense that the person does not deserve happiness. If we are guilty, we think we deserve punishment. This makes us feel uneasy when we are happy or enjoying ourselves because we feel the other shoe may fall. If we deserve punishment, we certainly do not deserve happiness. Thus, we have a conflict between wanting to feel enjoyment, pleasure and happiness and feeling like we do not want it based on our fears. All sorts of compromises then go on in the personality. Instead of winning, we might mysteriously find that we get anxious and slow down our efforts at an activity in the final moments in order to come in second place. We may procrastinate so much that we are always a little late for things, so even if we succeed at some activities or accomplishments, we draw enough criticism to create worry that we might be rejected or shamed.

Since we feel guilty about this unconscious negativity, it follows that real self-esteem suffers. It is hard to have good self-esteem if you feel deep down that you are bad because of your anger, resentment, spite, envy and the like. We just do not feel good about ourselves when we harbor these feelings and attitudes. We may try to talk ourselves into feeling good about ourselves, but we never fully succeed. We may try to accomplish great things, but that does not really work either. We may read self-esteem books that have us use positive visualization to create self-esteem and a positive picture of ourselves. These activities help our self-esteem, but they amount to a sort of superimposition of good feelings over bad, and sometimes even create more anxiety when we have not worked through the deep feeling that we are guilty and undeserving of good things in life. This feeling of low self-esteem and badness also leads to the next element of the vicious circle, which is actively courting negative experience.

Seeking Punishment

A common solution to this low self-esteem and need for punishment is to "beat others to the punch." There is a certain shame and helplessness that comes from feeling badly about ourselves and fearing life will punish us at any second. We cope sometimes by the solution of "If I punish first, I can at least have a modicum of dignity by taking the sword out of the other's hand and bringing the punishment on myself. At least then I have a sense of self-agency and a feeling of being captain of my own ship."

When this strategy is employed, we may become the first to discredit ourselves. We will be the first to criticize. We will castigate ourselves, sometimes even in public, so that the other person does not do it first. Sometimes we even laugh at ourselves and our accomplishments to ward off the sword from falling. The famous "gallows laugh" is an expression of this dynamic; it is the laugh we sometimes have when misfortunes befall us. We laugh at ourselves, which is our way of going with the punishment. We split ourselves, and one part laughs in concert with the punishment, even though we are truly a victim of an injury at the same time.

Seeking punishment also takes the form of constant worry, fear of attack or suffering over any neurotic symptom. As Freud noted, all the neurotic fears and depressive symptoms may mysteriously disappear when physical illness befalls a person. This sort of functioning reminds me of the fable *The Pied Piper of Hamlin*. The magical Piper led the children away from Hamlin, where they were never heard from again. The reason he led the children away was that he had previously led the rats away from the town and was promised a fee, which the mayor reneged on. The piper got his revenge when payment was not made. "Someone has to pay the piper" is the famous moral of the story. The fable is illustrative of how someone or some symptom has to be offered in payment. I often say to clients who develop a new symptom or have an exacerbation of an old symptom after some improvement that "someone has to pay the piper." It is interesting to note that in one major version of the fable, three children are saved from the piper, all of whom are infirm. One is crippled and cannot follow quickly enough, one is blind and cannot find his way, and one is deaf and cannot hear the piper. According to my hypothesis, they have already paid the piper by their infirmities.

Paranoid Projection

In depth psychology, we typically think of projection as the placing of feelings we cannot accept in ourselves onto other people. I think this is true as an overview for simple explanatory purposes. A more profound explanation is that projection is actually an unconscious assumption that everyone else really feels deep down the negative feelings we cannot accept in ourselves. If we are contemptuous, we feel others are contemptuous toward us. If we are judgmental, we feel others judge us. If we are jealous of others, we feel they will be jealous of us. If we envy people's good qualities, we fear others will begrudge us ours. If we are really angry and harbor murderous rage, as in the case of paranoid schizophrenia, we feel others want to murder us. The equation is clear: that whatever negativity we cannot face in ourselves, own and work through, we fear the same negativity is aimed at us. This projection of our anger and faults, such as envy and jealousy, which occur due to childhood hurts, is another link in the Promethean chain that recurrently keeps us bound to a belief in a world that will begrudge us any advancement, positive feelings or self-care.

Compulsive Dependency

The final problematic fate that anchors the Promethean chain is *compulsive dependency*. Because of previous links in the chain, we need more reassurance from others since we feel others are resentful of our achieving good things. And because of our unconscious guilt, self-punishment and low self-worth, we become doubly and triply dependent on others to like us, reflect our value, be interested in us and esteem and love us to assuage our self-doubt. Hence, our dependency gets further and further out of hand, and we are back at the point where we started. We are now more like children who are very dependent on love and approval from others for their sense of well-being rather than like mature, independent adults. Once again, we have unmeetable dependency demands, which cause more anger and resentment and perpetuate the cycle of self-defeat that forms the last link in the Promethean chain.

It is important to note that I do not advocate a counterdependent attitude as an ultimate goal. A counterdependent attitude leads one to feel that any sort of healthy dependency, or need for others, means we are weak or a failure. This counterdependent attitude usually bespeaks the opposite extreme, which is compulsive dependency. A healthy interdependency is the goal, whereby one feels a need for others and the benefits that being a social person provide as well as has the ability to accept non-gratification without feeling outrage and requiring punishment of others who do not meet our needs.

Treatment Overview

In therapy, I often work psychoeducationally with the Promethean chain. I do discuss with patients the nature of unconscious aggression and unconscious guilt in rhythm with the disclosure of their problems in a manner that is relevant to them. I also discuss the importance of their being able to accept all their feelings and wishes, even unflattering ones. I try to build up their ability to self-reflect on these issues without self-recrimination and moralization. I attempt to build up their ability to entertain and contain the negative within themselves. In addition, I discuss with them that any negativity is really confused positivity—love outraged and distorted. I point out that our core is benevolent and wants good for ourselves and others and knows the value of that, but psychic pain and injury and confusion cause negative and even cruel impulses in us that shrouds the core self, which needs to be contained, understood and transformed. I call this the *low self* that covers our core.

Case Example 1

A patient enters treatment for a crippling obsessive–compulsive disorder and depression. He is very bright but has had only limited vocational success and poor relationships throughout his life. He never feels deserving of anything and fights what he calls his "self-sabotage," which is his tendency to avoid anything good for himself and an impulse to wreck positive strivings. He often believes that if he feels like telling someone off, he has done so and forgotten. He then worries irrationally that he has injured the person and also fears reprisal. He feels the same about a desire to hit a person. He always fears that he has already done so. In an effort to help him, his previous therapists have told him that "This is not you; this is the OCD." This has had only minimal success for him. It does help him feel he is okay, at least consciously, and he is always fighting the feeling that he is really a horrible, evil and cruel person.

Those therapies that try to build people up with a superimposition of support over their terrible unconscious guilt always have only a partial measure of success. Clients often think, "If they really knew me, they wouldn't think I was a good person." I take an almost opposite approach. For example, I asked this person to tell me one of his obsessions. He talked of feeling that he had hit his neighbor because he imagined he had. He said, "I would never want to do that. That is the OCD."

> Franklin: "Oh, yes, you would. Maybe not in your heart of hearts, but you are human and we have angry feelings as humans."
> Patient: "I don't know about that."
> Franklin: "Tell me more about it. Were you upset about something with her?"
> Patient: "Oh yeah, she is one of the neighbors who feeds these birds in our neighborhood, which shit all over everything. My wife tells her off and chases the birds away and now all the neighbors hate me and stare me down."
> Franklin: "So, you are not mad at this woman?"
> Patient: "I don't know if I'm mad. I don't like it."

Franklin: "I think you are mad as hell at her and want to smack her a good one. You see, you confuse feelings with actions. You can have all kinds of feelings you may never act on. You do with your feelings what is most constructive for you at a given moment, but pretending you don't feel something is going to cause these OCD problems even more."

Patient: "Really?"

Franklin: "Yes! A lot of people would want to smack a neighbor like that. I'm not saying you should even say anything to her necessarily, but don't kid yourself that you aren't mad at her and wouldn't like to smack her. That is why you worry you have already done it, because you want to do it."

Patient: (laughs) "Oh, maybe." (The laughter is a good sign that a patient has felt the zest in the aggression. The pleasure in the aggressive feelings must be felt at some point for true liberation because what patients fear the most is their pleasure in being mean or aggressive.)

Franklin: "It's good you laugh. Can you feel it a little?"

Patient: "Yeah, I guess I can."

This was the beginning of steady improvement for this patient. He began to accept himself deeply with his aggression and pleasure in his anger, and with the idea that this was not who he ultimately was but rather an element of himself he needed to accept. This is different than telling a patient that he is good and is not really angry, and that those foreign feelings are just the disease talking.

Case Example 2

A patient I have seen for a number of years is struggling with projection of his unconscious aggression and unconscious guilt. He is an artist and is finally able to enter shows and sell his art. He knows he is frightened of doing so and thinks people will hate him if he is successful. After having a discussion with his sister, he tells me he is angry at her for always using him as her counselor and putting him between her and other family members. This is great for him and a major therapeutic advancement that he can freely acknowledge that he is angry. What I notice, though, is that he does not have much of an affective resonance. He seems to report his anger sort of like he is reading a newspaper or talking about someone else. Near the end of the session, I see he has a somewhat intellectualized acceptance of his feelings but not a deeply felt sense. This not feeling his feelings deeply seems to be his next edge for growth that needs to be worked with to help set him free.

> Patient: "I am angry at my sister. She always comes over and tells me for hours how bad my mother is and my family. I felt like telling her, 'Hey, they feel the same way toward you.' I did manage to tell her something like that later as we talked."
>
> Franklin: "That's good you could at least talk to her and voice somewhat of a complaint. I notice, though, as you talk, it is like you don't really resonate with this feeling of anger. It is as if you are talking about someone else."
>
> Patient: "Oh. I didn't know I did that."
>
> Franklin: "Yes. What I would like you to do is to feel it in your body. Let yourself feel it in your hands and arms and back. I would like you to do this with all your feelings. Go toward them, not away from them. Try to approach it like actors do with method acting. Try to tune into your feelings whenever you notice them. Try to feel them fully in your body; stay with them for a while. I would like you to try to feel the pleasure and excitement in your anger, too. This will help you if you can learn to do this. I would like you to do this every day now."
>
> Patient: "Okay, I will try that."
>
> Franklin: "Yes, please try every day."

I focused on this affect tolerance because liberation from unconscious guilt and negativity does not just come from an intellectualized understanding of it but rather a felt, alive sense of where one derives pleasure from the negative feeling. When this happens and feelings are felt deeply and contained bodily and the person does not feel he is horribly bad for doing this or needing to act out these feelings, liberation from guilt and negativity moves forward.

Feelings are not actions. Containment comes first, and by witnessing and recognizing the negative affect over time, the psychic distance and evaluation of these negative emotions begins to degrade them. We develop a sense of, "Isn't that silly? I am doing it again." Then the feelings soften and actually transform, as a deeper place in us knows we feel better to be loving rather than negative. We now do this without repressing the feelings, which is no solution at all to truly transform feelings, but by gradually changing them.

Case Example 3

Another patient had trouble with anything positive happening in her life and was terribly anxious with even supportive comments I would make about her. She would almost beg me to verbally abuse her in treatment. I think my caring attitude was the sword of Damocles that she wanted to be rid of. In dreams, she would think of kittens and bunnies being mutilated and destroyed. I asked her for her associations, and she discussed how she loved bunnies and kittens and had a pet kitten that she loved more than anything in the world. She also felt she would do anything to protect these vulnerable beings. As her associations continued, it seemed apparent the kittens and bunnies represented both that which she loved most dearly and also the longing and vulnerable element in her that wanted positive, loving beings in her life. This she wanted to kill because it made her too vulnerable and chained her to desire to love and be loved. This has led to torment in her life, especially in childhood when she was severely and cruelly abused. Her warm, loving, tender longings had, as Henry Krystal would say, *heralds of impending traumatic feelings.*

Interpreting this to her over time and helping her get used to her more positive feelings has helped her become more loving and self-caring. It is always a battle though—two steps forward and one step back. That the work is a battle is an apt description. In fact, it is more than a battle; it is like a military campaign. I find when people move to a higher level of functioning in their lives—more fulfillment, better self-care, more success in their lives and better love relationships— it always takes time. All of the Promethean elements create a great resistance to holding ground that has been gained in the work of liberation. The guilt, the fear due to projections, the lower self-attitude that love and surrender is a trap—all conspire to make it difficult for clients or those engaged in transformation work to hold ground they have gained. They move forward, get anxious and tend to fall back into more self-defeating ways. People actually have to get used to feeling better. Our old way of being causes a habit pattern that tends to stay in place—Freud's *Id resistance* or a pull in the unconscious to stay attached to our problems. It takes time and dosing ourselves with the anxiety of past hurts and fear of change to work through our old attachment to negative situations and internalized condemning relationships. The analogy to a military campaign and ground gained and occasionally lost, I believe, helps people deal with the inevitable setbacks and relapses on the way to the liberation of the core self.

Further Comments on Technique

As I suggested earlier, every technique commonly used in depth psychotherapy is appropriate, including analysis of transference and resistance, examination of reenactment of childhood hurts in the therapeutic relationship, interpretation of unconscious wishes and their defenses and so forth. Approaches I suggest that are a bit different than classic psychodynamic psychotherapy, are: 1) looking for unhealthy needs and needs in conflict, attempting to affirm and induce healthy needs in ourselves, 2) interpreting the false, defensive, idealized personality masks that shroud the core self, 3) finding the benign traits within the negative in our personality, 4) strengthening the ego with the goal to not simply regulate the unconscious but to surrender the ego to our core self with its intuitive wisdom, 5) analyzing and unbinding the Promethean chains of self-defeat that trap us, 6) embracing a felt sense of emotions, their containment and transformation and 7) keeping our eyes on the prize of liberating the spiritual and divine core self with its wonderful, benevolent and creative properties as the ultimate goal of the work, instead of merely resolving a psychological problem. Below I list some further techniques that may be of help. These are unusual techniques that I have developed through years of experience in mystical schools and as a psychoanalyst/psychologist.

The Mourning Liberation Process

The mourning liberation process is often a labor-intensive process, taking weeks and months to free the positive affect that is contained within negative affect. To dose a person with affective experience in such a way that his or her tolerance and regulation gain the upper hand and allow the transformation from negative to positive affective experience to take place requires tact and sensitivity. As treatment progresses, however, and one is able to tolerate and regulate affect, the experience can be accelerated, and even in one session a critical degree of affect transformation may take place. For example, on one occasion I was leading a group that included a man who was very frightened of relationships with women. During one group, he therapeutically ventilated his rage at a particular woman. He ranted as she stood in front of him, "You bitch, you nasty bitch, I hate you and every one of you. You stand there and are smug and cut off. I hate you so much." Then he broke down and began to cry. You could see him melt into softer feelings, which were very hard for him to handle. As he cried he began to say over and over again, "You are so beautiful, it hurts. I can't handle it. You are just so beautiful, so beautiful" He sobbed and sobbed. It was visible that he was able to make a profound feeling connection to and appreciation for this woman, who seemed to be emblematic of all women to him. The breakthrough from his separateness into a rapturous, amorous connection with this woman was very powerful but oddly difficult for him to experience. While it may have seemed easier when he was "melting" to disrupt these powerful feelings because they were so intense, at this moment it was important to simply support this movement to the positive core affect. As we all were able to stay grounded enough to tolerate the feelings, everyone was moved emotionally, and eventually a sense of calm and oneness seemed to overtake us.

This second phase of mourning, which liberates softer affect and pain from hard feelings and hard pain, contains within it a subprocess of surrender. This surrender is part of the work since it requires affect tolerance on the part of the client and analyst to remain supportive and stay with a positive mood, as softer affect and pain can bring up fears of being swept away or of losing oneself. Here analysts may often become frightened of the "rapture" of surrender and want to explain it away as defensive. While a moment of surrender does not denote a completed treatment or mean one does not have issues to be dealt with, it is nonetheless a positive, life-affirming soul movement. Emanuel Ghent (2002), defines surrender in part thusly: "It may be accompanied by a feeling of dread and death, and/or clarity, relief, even ecstasy. Its ultimate direction is the discovery of one's identity, one's sense of self, one's sense of wholeness, even one's sense of unity with other living beings" (p. 111).

Another example is a fairly long first phase of treatment of experiencing negative affects and character faults, which led to a final phase of transformation and a melting into truly loving, ecstatic feelings. This patient was paraplegic with chronic pain. She had long felt bitter, suicidal and cheated by life. She also felt that there was a glass wall between her and life and that it caused her to be a spectator of her own existence. She "loved" her children because she knew she should, but she could not really feel it. After much work, she began to have feelings of guilt that she should have been a better mother to her children and that she should stop blaming her parents for her lot in life. She developed periods in which she just cried and wanted her children to have better lives than they did and prayed that they knew happiness that she had never experienced. She began to feel ecstatic—beyond herself. This all seemed strange and frightening to her. She stated that she did not know what was happening to her and she felt odd and puzzled by this felt sense of warm, positive feelings for her family and even her current caregivers. I stated, "What's happening is that after all this work, your heart is opening up. You have broken through the glass wall that you have always talked about, and you are really caring in much deeper ways and this is how it is coming to you. You are unthawing and your love is pouring out." Her response was to cry even more deeply and say, "I think that it's hard to stand. It feels so strong, I don't know what to do with myself." I responded, "Just feel it. You don't have to do anything. If you cry off and on for days, who cares?"

In subsequent sessions, she confirmed the sense that what she was feeling was love instead of craziness and that it was a major turning point in her life. She said to me in a deeply compelling way, "And you know what else? I so badly want to live now that I can't tell you; life feels so very meaningful to me. I feel so emotionally connected. I have never felt like this before." This affirmation and support led to a sense of surrender to positive affects that she previously felt were too strong to bear. Our work led to greater empathic relational abilities and an ecstatic sense of love and surrender to the wish for closeness and sense of union, which exists as loving capacities within each of our core selves. *The way to the other can be through the deepest longings of our inner selves.*

Emotional Dwelling

While the way to the other can paradoxically be found within our deepest self, the way to our deepest self can also be found in relational attunement with the other. Robert Stolorow (2014) brings forth the concept of *emotional dwelling*. In emotional dwelling, the helper actively participates in the pain or experience of the one being helped. It is not one mind "understanding" the other but actively participating in the pain or joy of the other in a way that does not shut it down but rather holds, embraces and lifts the pain/joy out of the background of consciousness. It is an active participation in the affects of another by tuning into a personal experience of analogous suffering or ecstasy and affirming it in a manner that calls the unbearable affects forth so they can be contained and metabolized. Many patients come into treatment and convey painful experiences that the therapist wants to reassure the patient about. Or even worse, the therapist tries to normalize or minimize the pain in an effort to comfort the patient. This usually ends in disaster, with the patient either foreclosing the experience or feeling misunderstood and never coming back.

The therapist needs to dwell with the patient in experiences that are hard to consciously contain, so that they have a chance to move through it. If you try to talk patients out of their suffering, they will try to convince you that you are wrong to see a silver lining in their troubles. If you stay with them in their pain and sorrow, they eventually and organically emerge with some capacity to organize themselves and gain a perspective on their suffering. Emotional dwelling is reminiscent of Carl Rogers' (1961) understanding of the person's frame of reference, but Stolorow tries to convey the power of suffering *with* a patient rather than solely understanding the patient from an external position. The distinction may appear subtle, but the difference is very often real. Emotional dwelling, with resonate experience and embracing the most difficult to embrace, has powerful emancipatory effects. We can only go there with another to the extent that we have embraced the most difficult and painful affects in ourselves.

Dying into Process

Dying into process is another aspect of this affective transformational work that leads to liberation of the core self. This is a dying into psychically painful feelings the patient has previously avoided. It is much like surrender, but surrender implies a giving over to something elementally positive while dying into may feel more like a loss of part of our identity. A patient was working on her abject dependency on others' favorable feelings for her in order to maintain a sense of well-being. In many ways, her psychic mortality felt dependent on others' acceptance of her. She felt she would simply die if I, as the analyst, and others in her life did not like and accept her. This seemed to accrue from an experience of shame, even mortification, when she was not affirmed. She would rather disappear into non-existence than face these feelings. She repressed the dynamic and converted it into anxiety. To counteract this, I encouraged her to allow her exquisite sensitivity to others to remain on the surface of her consciousness and feel the abject sense of shame and mortification as best as she could in each moment. I told her it would feel much like she was dying in these moments because she believed her sense of being a worthwhile, valuable and lovable human being was at stake. Only by feeling this over and over again and managing the feelings and realizing that she did not actually die, although she felt that she wanted to, would this begin to fade. This dying process reminds me of Otto Rank's (1973) fear of and longing for death as an avoidance of life. He, too, spoke of death as an embrace of unity and surrender. Although Rank never spoke of a unitive reality below or within our negative affect and experience, I would hope this is a technique he might have been fond of.

Playing with Aggression

A major element in transformation of negativity is its embrace and conscious containment in the person who is hoping to transform it. Interpersonally and in the therapeutic dyad the therapist must learn to survive the murderous thoughts, feelings and impulses of the client. Mike Eigen, in *The Sensitive Self* (2004c), discusses Wilfred Bion's formulation of freeing murder. Freeing murder is the play of very aggressive impulses in what D. W. Winnicott (1971) described as *transitional* or *potential space*. Potential space is a created space, in this case between psychotherapist and client, where psychic exchanges are seen as somehow imaginary and somehow paradoxically real. What is foundational in this potential space is that the client or therapist owns the aggressive impulse and takes responsibility for it as a problem or issue but still is able to communicate the impulse in a playful way.

The effect of playing with aggression is to give more profound emotional permission to experience the aggression in a safe way, a way that can be used to work over and through the aggression. For example, a patient is afraid of her aggressive impulses and worries that if she comes in contact with an adolescent, she will want to hurt him or her. As she talks about the fear of hurting the adolescent, I make the abstract thought very concrete and say, "So you want to punch the girl, huh?" The patient smiles and says, "Well, I don't know about that." I reply, "Yeah, that may be too easy. If you had a hammer it would be better; you could really clobber her." The patient laughs quite a bit as I say this, which to me demonstrates that it freed up her murderous impulse a little within this frame of being playful about it.

In another case, a client, who is rather schizoid with very blunted affect, began talking about the movie *Raging Bull* starring Robert De Niro. He was reviewing the scene in which De Niro's character, Jake

LaMotta, was beating up his brother. My client was laughing out loud as he described the beating that was delivered. I smiled and chuckled with him, then told him, "I am so glad that can enjoy your anger with this movie. I have never seen you so animated." He smiled and continued to review and laugh about the movie.

Still another client is afraid she will hurt kids if they come into a public restroom. She says, "There are all kinds of ways I could hurt them. I could flush them down the toilet or even drown them in the sink, you know?" I said, "I think the toilet is much better." She then laughed a lot. This seemed to give her permission to talk about her angry feelings in detail. She went on to discuss her hatred of children's preciousness as they long to be enjoyed and long for love. I said, "That is precisely where you are wounded. Your mother never cared about your tender longings and vulnerability. She never enjoyed you. You hate it when you see it in others, and you hate the tender child inside." This dialogue opened the door wide for a growth spurt in the transformation of her hatred.

With someone who is more in touch with their anger but does not feel the pain of it or understand the pain of the victim, I might try to tease out and embrace the guilt or pain that is absent. Each situation, client and moment is different, and the therapist must use her or his intuition as what is absent or repressed, if anything, that needs to emerge for transformation to occur.

The aggression often needs to emerge in the therapeutic relationship as transference or enactment. An example of playing with aggression in the transference is the case of a client who said, "I am so mad at you, I could spit." I said, "You mean cut off my head and spit down my throat?" She said, "Yeah, that too." In this case, I read that the client's anger harbored murderous impulses she could not accept and contain but that she was somewhat ready to hear about them. In another case with someone with whom I did not have a well-developed therapeutic relationship established, I may have said nothing but rather patiently contained what she had already said without being reactive to her or defensive. The therapist's intuition about the client's capacity for containment of aggressive play always has to be the guide for these types of interventions to be useful. As therapists mature in their role as therapist, their intuitive capacities also mature, as well as the confidence to play with aggression.

I do these types of interventions because they can be very important in the psychotherapeutic approach to growth. Without them or other active affective interventions, clients will often rest with an intellectualized understanding of their "problematic" affect, which may create a therapeutic deadness. Emotions of any type need to be felt deeply and continually for real emotional growth to mature. Knowing one's feelings is different than owning and experiencing them. Faith in our resonate capacities to contain affect grows as affects are truly registered and felt.

Affirming the Core Self

Affirming the existence of the core self and that its loving qualities are who a patient really is in his or her heart of hearts can make tolerable the negative transference and negative affective states that seem otherwise unbearable. A particular patient, despite repetitive sessions, could not shake the hate he felt for me, even though we both knew he valued me highly. One way in which he experienced this hate was by way of the transference in perceiving I was tired and that I was withholding from him by not having as much energy. He would become very angry and feel I was neglecting him and rant at me for it. He also hated me because I had a good life and he did not, and he felt I was born with a silver spoon. He had fantasies of wanting to cut me up, torture me and burn me alive. Eventually, he could hardly stand all the hate he felt and wondered whether he should stop analysis. I was worried about him and all the self-loathing he had that caused him to feel so hateful. He was in a great deal of pain. Wondering how I could help moderate his pain, tolerate his cruelty and sustain the analysis, I reframed his cruelty as a distortion of longing for love and concern from me.

I said to him: "All this hate is not the real you. You were deeply injured as a child and you felt utterly alone, and now you want to make sure I am not going to gyp you like your parents did. You also want to burn me alive to externalize all your pain and have me feel the pain you have felt for a change. This is a way to cope with your pain and try to change your history by punishing me. It can't work because the past is the past, but please don't think this is just a character trait of yours that you were born with. You were born with a longing for love and fulfillment like the rest of us, but you had a lot of pain that caused you to feel cruel. Your pain that you register when you feel angry with me is also from the place in you that feels deeply connected with me. The core of you where you don't want to hurt me and are distressed by these feelings is the loving you, and I am okay even with your anger. If you stay with your authentic feelings, your love will increase and, eventually, much of your cruelty will fade away." "God, I hope so" he cried with a mixture of sadness and pleading. "I get so sick of myself that I can't stand it." This led to a sense of emotional softening in this session, and we could feel a greater sense of self-acceptance emerging.

As sessions passed, by reframing his anger in terms such as this, his inner cruelty faded and his self-esteem and loving capacities overtook his cruelty. Perhaps this might have happened if I had not reframed his cruel feelings as love outraged. But my sense at the time, besides simply wanting him to feel better, was that if I did not I might have lost him as he could not stand himself because of his cruelty. The work led to greater empathic relational abilities and surrender to the wish for closeness and sense of union that exist as loving capacities within the *core self* in each of us. Again, it emphasizes that the way to the other is through the deepest longings of our inner selves.

Transforming Duality

Similar to but perhaps broader than the "dying into" process is the *transforming duality process*. It is different than simple mindfulness or being in the moment practices in that it points at our deepest psychological fears and anxieties and aims at their transformation. Unlike most schools of psychology, most esoteric spiritual schools consider fear to be a fault or a problem, not simply an effect of a neurosis or psychosis. This is so because fear keeps us from the unitive state and the divine. One cannot be at peace if one is afraid. Fear exists in the state of duality, not unity. To be at rest in unity one must basically learn to transcend fear. This cannot be done by repressing fear, or any fault or problem, but by consciously containing the fear and attempting to use it as a stepping stone toward the liberation process.

How does one do this? We always tend to run from negative situations, pushing and straining to avoid them. We run from our fear of death, the passage of time, the unpleasant in many forms. This causes a strain in the personality, a tension and a desire to avoid life with all its ups and downs. The way beyond this straining and fear is to take each problem, each pratfall, each difficulty that life gives us as a stepping stone to self-examine what we need to do to change ourselves as best we can so the problems do not need to return. Or, if they do return, we can handle them, including the great existential fear of death. People have gone through this gateway forever and will continue to do so. Displeasure, pain and frustration are part of life, but when these feelings are not repressed or cringed from but contained and accepted, we move toward living beyond fear and begin to taste more and more a state where everyday existential fears of living and dying fade into a vanishing point.

This is a lifelong process, but if practiced continually, almost daily, over time life becomes peaceful. Fear, terror and a host of negative effects that result from the fear abate as well. This is quite tricky. The natural tendency is to repress fear and then believe we do not have it until the next problem arises. Or to simply say, "Of course, we have fear all the time, so what does this add to my sense of peace or well-being?" I say that if the unitive state is pointed at as the ideal and our daily existential fears are not run from but at least the attempt is made to accept them, it will pay dividends over time even though the ideal state of basic fearlessness will probably never be achieved totally.

As therapists, we can encourage this practice of facing fear and giving up the struggle to run away from it and life's difficulties rather than using fear and difficulties as teachers and guides to self-transformation. As honest spiritual searchers, we can practice this ourselves. Anyone who has the psychological mindedness to pick up this book has the capacity to apply this concept. Many clients may not want to use it or find it too esoteric, but those who seek a spiritual/psychological liberation from duality should find it helpful.

In classic depth psychology, everything in our dreams is our own creation. Dream elements and figures are a combination of wish and defense against the wish in disguise. For example, a common nightmare is that of a monster or some sort of malevolent figure chasing us, from which it is hard to escape. Sometimes in the dream we run but do not gain any distance on the monster. Most people think the monster is some sort of accidental occurrence or a metaphor for something scary going on in one's life. While the monster as a metaphor of a life event may bear some truth, it is a thin reading of the dream elements. The monster is rather something aggressively monstrous in oneself, or at least the conscious self assumes it to be. The fact that one cannot escape from it represents aggression that is turned on oneself because of unconscious guilt and need for self-punishment. A dream of this nature is always an outpicturing of intrapsychic conflict. The same can be said of one's life. Based on the notion of radical self-responsibility, everything we create in our lives is an outpicturing of what is healthy and unhealthy in our personality. Some people always spoil their relationships or pick bad partners to begin with. This is not an accident. Some do well professionally but can never get over the hump or get ahead and wonder why they made that bad decision or unwise investment. This is because something in the soul is unready for the responsibility of the accomplishment, the success or the fulfillment based on the Promethean complex or some other "no" to fulfillment in the soul. These problems that just "seem to befall us" are often what we are afraid of in life and strain away from in fear. With this approach, I am suggesting we turn this process on its head and ask ourselves, "What lesson is life trying to teach us?" For example, if a person is upset over a business failure, we might examine what led him to make this or that decision. Did he enter the business venture with his eyes shut about the true honesty of a business partner? Did he hope for too much from the partner in spite of clues to the contrary? Did he try to force life to fit his expectations instead of seeing the reality? Was the client really committed, and did he put the proper amount of time and money into the enterprise so that it could succeed?

The same example could apply to an illness. How well are we taking care of ourselves? How well are we eating, exercising and so forth? Are we pushing and straining in life, creating a cascade of toxic catecholamines and neuroregulators that make us ill? If so, why? And what can we do about it? What may we need to grieve to give up this struggle? What pathogenic beliefs are involved? What Promethean chain is binding us to the proverbial rocks and unleashing Pandora's torments?

If the problems in our life are looked at as teachers, gifts and advice from life to correct something amiss in our soul, then we begin to approach a life in a unitive way. If we try to let go of the fear without repression but a calm affirmation daily that the bad can be good and the good can have bad results, we taste unitive consciousness. Be careful not to approach this glibly by just paying lip service to the concept. It takes practice when problems emerge to express a positive affirmation to life constantly and for our desire to live beyond duality to slowly emerge as a way of being in the world.

This reminds me of a story about a Native American Shaman who was trying to teach non-duality. I cannot remember it exactly, but I remember the lesson enough to recreate it here.

Shaman: " I got a new horse a few weeks ago.

Apprentice: "Oh, that's good."
Shaman: "No. I fell off a few days later and broke my arm."
Apprentice: "Oh, that's bad."
Shaman: "No, because my arm was broke, I didn't plant the crop which would have been drowned out a couple of days later."

We could go on with the story, but many of us can see the parallel in our own lives. One obvious example for me was when I received a little inheritance, which I thought was really nice. It ended up causing so many family problems that, it was not good at all, and I ended up wishing I had never received it. A second example was when I accidently let my psychology license expire. This caused a great deal of financial problems, which I thought were terrible. It turns out that

I discovered a new kind of license provider number I could apply for that opened up all kinds of potentially lucrative business opportunities. We will see how successful it really is in the long run.

Even our own death and those of loved ones we cherish so much can be accepted. Although we hate this thought, death is not the ultimate definition of who we are. Like many others, I believe in the transmigration of the soul and that death is a new door to life. I also know that despite my conviction I am afraid of the great existential death. Even true believers do not want to die to get to heaven. Hence, I need to try to practice what I am preaching here daily. If you are not a believer, like many of my existentialistic friends, then you still need to learn how to deal with your mortality, and I suggest that practicing non-dualistic thinking would be helpful.

Relationship as a Measure of an Individual's Spiritual and Psychological Health and its Use in Growth Dynamics

Love one another but make not a bond of love: let it rather
be a moving sea between the shores of your souls.
~ Khalil Gibran

The quality of our relationships can be a gauge of our emotional and spiritual maturity and, alternatively, our inner conflict. Relationships are powerful generators of health, benevolence and joy and, conversely, pain, struggle and conflict. That relationship brings out the worst and the best of us points to its practical use as a yardstick for the level of our inner emotional health or lack thereof.

When we as parents, children, lovers or friends unconsciously harbor negative demands and attitudes toward others in relationship, we begin to spin a web in which we become ensnarled. If we expect other people to capitulate to our will and demands in any way, then deep down we believe other people have the right to expect capitulation from us. The snare has been set and now we fear deep emotional involvement in relationship because it feels like an *involuntary commitment,* or perhaps worse. When we expect capitulation from those we "love," deep relating becomes in our unconscious an invitation to be enslaved.

Many of us, at least at times, kid ourselves about the quality of our relationships. Because of the ubiquitous use of denial in the human personality, many live under the illusion that their relationships are perfectly fine when in reality they are mostly superficial and lack aliveness. By superficial, I mean lacking in depth of emotional connection and a lack of real appreciation for the needs, wants, fears and longings of the other person—the other's subjectivity. Relationships that are superficial lack that "I–thou" quality, as discussed by Martin Buber (1996). When relationships are superficial, the other is either not appreciated or primarily treated as an object to meet the needs of the superficial relater. The partner or friend is just not profoundly and meaningfully invested in and can be easily given up or traded for someone else. Someone who has the capacity for deeper relating will be able to represent the other as a subjective self, not simply an extension of him- or herself.

Sometimes we may safeguard our illusion that we are doing well in relationship by withdrawing from relationship. We hide out in single life or distant friendship. When we get lonely, we may either point fingers at others as the cause of why we have had to withdraw, or we simply kid ourselves that loneliness is a better choice or that we do not really want relationships. When we withdraw from relationship with a sour grapes attitude toward others by pretending relationship is not important or needed, it is easier to maintain the illusion that we have worked out all the trouble that comes through closeness.

For those of us who employ superficiality or withdraw as a defense, when a deeper relationship emerges all hell may break loose. With the emergence of greater closeness, deeper feelings of longing, need and dependency emerge, as does anger. Wilfred Bion (2004) described this dynamic as *angry dependency*. Anger intensifies as needs intensify because when deeper needs and longings are evidenced but are not always met, people become frustrated. They are frustrated with the lack of gratification, whereas before they could more easily contain their need and anger when relationship was more superficial. Sometimes, long-buried dependency and anger create open conflict and hostility or admixtures of blame and withdrawal from the relationship. At this point, it becomes difficult to self-reflect and discover one's own contribution to a relationship conflict.

The fear of love and closeness may come as a surprise to those who are not familiar with the conflictual nature of the human personality that we find in depth psychology, but it is an extremely important point. We all fear love to greater or lesser degrees even though we simultaneously long for it. Many of us think, of course, that we *only* long for love. Everyone wants it, needs it and longs for it. To the psychologically unsophisticated, the longing for love is the alpha and omega of human psychology. That we fear love and do not want it in some measure often seems counterintuitive. But we do fear it, avoid it and at times even want to kill it because it seems like a herald of danger, deadness or a fate worse than death—an entrapment in a living death. We fear love for many reasons. If we unconsciously are demanding, possessive and punishing, we fear that demandingness, possessiveness and punishment is what others will mete out to us under the guise of love. To the extent that we labor under the spell of any character fault such as vanity, hubris, envy, jealousy, demandingness, angry dependency, we will feel we do not deserve love. If we really do become close to someone, they will attack us with similar character issues. We always assume that others are like our worst faults, even if our faults are unconscious to us and we act very kindly to others in a false self, "mask-like" way. Therefore, if we become close and passionately attached to others, "in love" as it were, we are really in danger of the worst kind of torments rearing their ugly heads.

Even those of us who fortunately have never been endowed with these more basic character faults to any great extent may still fear love. These more fortunate types may simply not be ready to offer the same kind of patience, forgiveness and allowance for others' aggression as they expect to receive themselves. There is an exacting measure in ourselves that knows we can only stand as much love as we are prepared to give. As we forgive, so shall we feel we deserve forgiveness. As we allow others their mistakes or minor aggressions without punishing them, so do we feel deserving of allowance from others. As we give, so shall we receive.

When relationships are of the false-self variety, feelings may begin to become blunted or numbed over time. Only by self-reflection on how we mask our demands, expectations, anger and so on can we drop our false presentation in relationship and begin to live more authentically and feel the vitality that authentic relating brings, as well as the safety of a deep, loving relationship.

It is so easy to externalize blame in relationship. Common externalizations of blame in and avoidance of relationship are: my partner is too demanding, too needy, too controlling, wants too much from me, expects too much from me, and so forth. The persons doing the judging most often have the same faults within themselves as they are projecting outward and for which they are blaming the other. When we lack patience, self-composure, the ability to be alone, the ability to tolerate frustration and to be outpouring with love and acceptance, when we are an empty cup that demands to be filled, then to that exact extent we fear relationship.

Any relationship that is approached from an either/or prospective or black-and-white perspective begs for trouble. It is always the case that there are two people involved when relationships are conflictual. Even in a very lopsided relationship, where one person in the relationship is obviously abusive or controlling, there is still something in the "victim" who engages with the negativistic person that needs to be examined, understood, and worked through. Then a fuller release from negative relating can take place so that a deeper loving relating becomes possible.

Usually, those with less emotional and spiritual maturity tend to do the lion's share of the blaming in a relationship. If we want to grow emotionally, instead of blaming the emphasis should be on examining oneself. That does not mean one should not be assertive and ask for what one needs in a relationship. It is healthy to have positive expectations and healthy needs, but that is different than blaming, attacking, accusing and demanding more from your partner than you are willing to give. When we are demanding, controlling or manipulative, whether we are aware of it or not, it affects the other. They will fight back or rebel, even if only inwardly by withdrawing.

Guilt manipulation is another major tactic the emotionally immature use to blame the other in relationship. When people cannot be honest about their demands, neediness or blame, they sometimes default to guilt tripping the other as a way to blame them and whitewash their own faults. This is an insidious form of hostility that masks their own low-self demands, aggression and blame. It adds insult to injury when they guilt trip the other. They may have their own angry, dependent demands but instead of owning their demands, they blame the other for refusing them. This whitewashes their faults and accuses the other simultaneously. When this guilt tripping happens, the blame game goes on and on, with reactions and counterreactions in the form of a vicious circle. This often culminates in the breakdown of the relationship.

Another common form of guilt manipulation we often employ is the overdramatization of hurt. Overdramatizing an injury to make the other feel guilty and badly as a way to coerce change is an insidious form of manipulation that ultimately causes fear of closeness. If you play up hurts to injure and guilt the other, you will feel bound by similar guilt manipulation. Unconsciously, we register that if we expect the other to bend to our guilt manipulation, then we should bend to their guilt manipulation as well. All this guilting back and forth between partners in relationship usually happens relatively unconsciously, with both parties caught in the snare of guilt and resentment.

Tony comes into therapy with anxiety and depression. His girlfriend is unhappy with him for his crabbiness and dysphonic mood. She wants a happier guy. He wonders himself why he is so anxious, guilt ridden and crabby. Tony is chronically angry at his girlfriend when she "takes too long" to do something, like shop, be with her friends or talk on the phone. Conversely, he was always anxious when he was late, took too long or was not present enough. The answer to his wondering was found in his vicious circle. He felt trapped by his fear of losing her affection and angry that she would not remain constant for him emotionally and physically. There was a connection between his anger and his dependency. As Tony was able to challenge himself on his demandingness, tolerate the frustration of his girlfriend's absence and not punish her for her independence, he was able to tolerate separation. He began to feel more free to be separate himself and would reassure himself with the phrase, "If I can tolerate her taking time for herself and being separate, maybe I don't have to be so afraid of taking time for myself and being separate." The more he could identify his demandingness, guilt manipulation and punishing attitude for his girlfriend's independence, the more independent he became—or, more correctly stated, the more healthily interdependent he became. Interdependence implies a healthy and relaxed tolerance of both closeness and separation.

In relationships between parents and children, guilt tripping can be seen from both the parent and children's side. Parents may imply or outright say, "You are killing me by being involved with that person." They may guilt trip children for desiring a romantic or sexual relationship, suggesting it is horrible for the burgeoning adult child to be romantic or sexually active. Aside from the guilting for sexual wishes and activity, the parents often wish to bind the child to them and forestall emancipation of the child. Parents most always have a conflictual relationship to their children's emancipation. They exuberantly exhort them to grow up and leave the nest while simultaneously undermining their gaining independence or moving on. Parents want to avoid the pain of separation, loss of their children's emotional presence and the vitalization of their lives that the children provide.

Children often attempt to manipulate parents through guilt. They become very injured and angry if one child receives something the other does not, even if the circumstances of the children differ. "How come Johnny gets to stay up later? How come Mary doesn't have to do the dishes? Why are you going out, I haven't seen you all day?" This may be uttered even when you have just spent the better part of a day together. These are common attempts to force parents to do the child's will, which parents have to learn to negotiate. Children and adults often have little conscious understanding that they are guilt tripping as a manipulation.   Still, especially in the adult-to-child paradigm, guilt manipulation can cause severe problems.

Sometimes people punish and guilt manipulate others by their own misery. They never can be happy because they believe if they are happy then the other person will not cater to their needs. They unconsciously have to be sick, suffering, burdened, worried and so on, so others will stay close and bend to their will. People with this issue have a pathogenic belief that others will only care about them if they are injured or in pain. They just do not believe anyone will care for them or take joy in being with them unless they bind the other through guilt. These types of guilt manipulators can never be happy for fear that others will abandon them if they are. The viscous circle goes on and on because the more they guilt manipulate others to be with them or care for them, the more others really do not want to be with them, even if they actually are. The guilt manipulator recognizes the resentment in the manipulated other and never feels satisfied because what he or she really wants is the joyous interest of the other rather than having to guilt the person into being there.

As is often evidenced in couple counseling, when a more mature person works on his or her side of an issue, even if the issue is smaller than that of the less mature person, it clears up the issue of how the more mature person is provoking some kind of reactivity in the other. The usual result is that the less mature person's problems become more conspicuous. These issues stick out in relief because it becomes obvious that he or she is not really being provoked, and it is harder to blame the other when there is no obvious provocation. The less mature person, then, is more compelled to work on him- or herself because the cited provocation is now gone from the relationship. This has the effect of pushing the less mature person to self-evaluate, and often the consequences of that self-evaluation and self-facing is that the psychic interaction of negativity further diminishes.

Another dysfunctional way to approach a relationship is, conversely, always to blame yourself for all the problems in your relationship. Habitually blaming oneself is tantamount to making oneself a doormat and invites the other person to wipe his or her feet on you. If you assume that you have no position, that you do not have a right to any needs and a right to want what you want, it will create a relational problem. Relating in this passive way gives the partner the impression that what he or she says, needs and wants is always right. This passively turning throat-up has the effect of making a monster out of one's partner. If the partner has no one to bounce up against, no one to push back or say "no," she or he begins to believe that her or his assumptions, wishes and criticisms are always right. The emboldened partner may become more and more tyrannical and entitled until the passive partner chooses to escape from the domination even while blaming him-or herself for escaping.

This overly passive way of approaching a relationship has to be corrected as well. However, it is very important not to go from one extreme to the other and become abusive or negativistic when making this correction, which, of course, is not easy. We have to learn to value our own beliefs, needs, wants and wishes. In short, we have to begin to value and believe in our own subjectivity, such that we honor that we have a place or a position in the world and that it is okay to want and need some things from the relationship. We need to also understand it is okay to assertive ourselves at times to get our needs met. Paradoxically, then, healthy relationships are marked by both assertiveness and surrender, but the assertiveness and surrender measured out have to be for the sake of love, not domination or passivity. Our intuition, which evolves as we mature emotionally, has to be the guide as to when to stand up and when to let go.

Underneath the passive position in a relationship often lurk severe active demands that the passive person has buried. You might say the demands simmer under the surface and actually cause passivity, as the passive person is afraid he or she will explode if these simmering demands are accessed. The passive person fears that the explosion of these demands will cause rejection or abandonment by the person to whom these demands are made, so they just bury them. Impatience, frustration, irritability, negativity, judgmentalness and so forth may simmer with great intensity. The more passive person may never have learned to modulate and express his or her aggression as assertiveness, and often fear, when analyzed, that taking an assertive position will cause him or her to become angry, abusive and destructive.

With this is kind of a duality between passivity and negativistic aggression, one needs to find the middle road. One's aggression, usually expressed in the form of control, demand, spite, envy, or hubris, must be contained, understood and modulated for relationship to work well. Through introspection and understanding, we can begin to grasp the underlying issues and needs that could ultimately be expressed in a positive manner. Once the work of introspection and self-facing begins, it does not mean that everything is going to come out right at first, but as time goes by sour notes improve and the inner music becomes more refined. We have to begin somewhere and, of course, in some sense, we have all already started the process of self- examination in relationship.

Perhaps the most profoundly transforming human relationship is the romantic relationship because it causes deeper longings and needs to spring forth than does any other type of relationship. This is due to the erotic drive, which creates deeper longing for intimacy, surrender and unity. The intensity of the romantic relationship also brings out more of our faults. Perhaps this is another reason why asceticism gained favor earlier in history as a choice for spiritual advancement. The ascetic seekers could manage the negative aspects of their personalities better and balance themselves more easily without the intense erotic drives involved. The emotional distance from passion that is achieved in asceticism may have allowed the ascetics to be greater teachers, helpers and spiritual directors for their followers. However, a layer of personality issues may have always been spiritually bypassed with this approach and never transformed.

If seeking ultimate unitive consciousness, spiritual bliss, peace and enlightenment, do not be fooled that you can find it living in a cave or on top of a mountain in actuality or in any symbolic form. The love between people is the greatest measuring stick of and tool for transformation that we, as humans, can find. Transformation through the crucible of relational functioning prepares us to accept greater and greater degrees of joy and happiness, which are preludes to a more transcendental kind of blissful experience. If bliss is not sought in this way, it will only be fleeting at best.

Deadness in any kind of relationship is another mark of problematic issues. When one does not feel eagerness, zest or joy in engaging in relationship, it is a testament that something is an issue in the personality. This is, again, especially true of romantic relationships. If unconscious negativism is covered over by a false self in the personality, deadness or numbness often occurs. Sometimes this is noted as inhibition of sexual desire in women or manifests as erectile dysfunction in men. If neither of these problems occurs at a clinical level, perhaps the sex life simply becomes rather routine or boring. This may often only be deeply corrected when the personality's false self is challenged and lower self emanations are understood and transformed.

It should be noted that the ego mind is a poor means to try to find your way between the dualities of relationship, such as when to give in, when to hold back, when to assert oneself, when to hold one's boundaries and so forth. The difficult negotiation of the complexities of relationship can only be solved with the enlistment of the intuitive, poetic and wise capacities of the core self. The ego can be used to help with determination and judgment, but it lacks the wisdom and inspired capacities to chart a wise course between the dualities. The ego usually looks for rules and laws, which are poor negotiators of the subtleties of the relational engagement. The heart actually has to be involved, as St. Paul might say, to understand morality and closeness and all the pratfalls that may occur when one is on the way toward a heartfelt surrender to unity in relationship. When the core self is engaged in the relationship, the lifestream, our passion and wisdom become involved, the flowing toward relationship becomes stronger and a passionate engagement and exuberant embrace of the ineffability of the other person is more common.

With regard to relationship, we are a self divided. The core self longs for union, unity and surrender, while our low self fights the longing for union. It fights closeness, unity and love in the mistaken belief that somehow it is better to remain a separate, isolated individual against others than to surrender to our deepest longing.

Out of ignorance and fear, the low self mistakenly works against its own ultimate bliss.

Because we are in conflict within ourselves regarding unity and closeness, it will always manifest in conflict externally between ourselves and other people. Until the inner conflict, or house divided, within us is transformed, our relationships will remain an outpicturing of our ambivalence. The inner conflict, with the ambivalent self for and against union, must be addressed by way of self-reflection, self-examination and tolerance of emotions that seem painful before ultimate union of a full self surrendered in union to the other can occur.

It may be hard to reorient the focus from the trouble externalized in the outer relationship to the corresponding element in oneself, but for a spiritually mature person this is the only way out of the trouble. The focus must be placed on any kind of disharmony that arises each day in a relationship and examined for character faults, selfishness, competitiveness, vanity, fear and shame of vulnerability that inhibit love in order for deep surrender to occur.

This does not mean one should indefinitely tolerate and work on negativistic, abusive, or hostile relationships. At some point, if either or both people are not willing to change and the spiritually mature person has examined and worked very hard on him- or herself, sometimes a relationship needs to be broken off and a new choice of partner or friend needs to be made. Still, emotionally mature persons will examine why they made the choice of that particular friendship or love relationship to begin with. They may then ask themselves why did they have their eyes wide shut, why did they not see what was there, or perhaps why did they choose someone so disharmonious? Was it because they felt they did not deserve more?

The treatment relationship between therapist/analyst and patient/client did not exist before the late 1800s. It is a unique laboratory relationship in which the therapy relationship itself is studied, as well as the dynamics of the patient's intrapsychic and unconscious process. In classical terms, we studied the role of transference and countertransference and what we called transference/countertransference binds, which is how transference and countertransference caused resistance and stalemates in psychotherapy. Those of a more Kleinian persuasion studied and worked with what is called *projective identification*—how the patient/client disowns some impulse or need in him- or herself, which causes the analyst/therapist to pick it up and act it out. It may be something akin to a client disavowing his or her own self-care because the client has an inhibition of conflict about self-care. Instead of pointing out that the conflict is the client's issue, the therapist may pick up one side of the conflict, in this case the healthy impulse for self-care, and exhort the client to care for herself, which in turn causes the client to resist the therapist's encouragement or exhortation.

The relational turn in psychoanalysis has emphasized the ongoing dyadic interplay of patient/analyst as a foundational status of treatment. The term *enactment* is now used to underline the equal status of patient and therapist as each brings his or her own subjectivity and unconscious process to the therapeutic dyad. The analyst is always encouraged to self-examine and find how he or she is involved in any therapeutic impasse, resistance, acting out, boundary issue and so forth. By extension, the idea is that the therapist becomes part of the problem before he or she becomes part of the solution. In classical vernacular, the patient develops a transference neurosis, in which the transference emerges as an ongoing pervasive dynamic in the therapeutic dyad. If the client had a depressed, dead-like, mother, the analyst is seen as depressed and dead, and interpretation of the transference neurosis is the main vehicle the analyst uses for therapeutic change.

In relational psychoanalytic work, the analyst examines his or her role in the dyadic interplay. Is the therapist in some way dead to the client? Has the therapist lost some of his or her zest in recent days? Is the therapist preoccupied in some way that resembles a depressed and unavailable mother? Has the therapist missed sessions, such that the patient feels emotionally abandoned by a depressed mother/analyst? If so, it is common for the therapist to apologize and make corrections to his or her mode of interaction, so that the client feels seen, heard and understood, thus suggesting the client has the power to take care of him- or herself in a dead relationship. It also brings awareness to the situation when the analyst sees, discusses and elaborates elements of the interaction of dead mother and angry/deprived client. The client may then mentalize and understand that the relationship difficulty occurs because the analyst has his own issues as well as the client's. The client may also employ new skills of affect tolerance and regulation, further freeing him or her from the vulnerability and pain of a dead or depressive relationship. Mentalization, empowerment, and affect regulation are not exhaustive of what happens in the working through of a relational enactment but are common outcomes.

Understanding the subjectivity of the other, both as unconscious and conscious processes, is also extremely important. Appreciating and valuing the client's needs, fears, wants, wishes, longings and imaginings is a rare event in many clients' lives, and something that a therapist needs to be good at for emotional, psychological and spiritual growth to occur. Valuing, supporting and encouraging the flourishing of the client's subjectivity are essential for the work. Sometimes, clients are afraid of elements of their subjectivity, so they repress them or defend against them in myriad ways. This often requires interpretation, clarification and confrontation of the client by the therapist to help elements emerge. At other times, a client may be conscious of elements of their personality that cause problems but either see them as virtues or as protective because they are syntonic.

An example of a problem that is seen as a virtue would be clients who suffer chronically by overworking themselves, not taking care of themselves and avoiding pleasurable activities in their lives. When this dynamic is brought out in the open, their retort might be, "This suffering is why I feel I have value. I am dedicated to others and deny myself for them. This is a good and valuable way to be in the world." This position may remain for a long time, until it is degraded by pointing out, again and again, the negative consequences of such a way of being in the world, and/or by pointing out the irrational belief that the only way to have value in this world is to chronically deny yourself pleasure and joy and to suffer. In relational work, learning to enjoy each other and the time together may be an important therapeutic approach.

An example of how a client may deny a healthy element of his or her subjectivity would be someone who avoids softness and caring impulses under the belief that if these caring impulses are embraced it will leave him or her vulnerable to exploitation by others. The belief that duality of caring equals vulnerability to exploitation versus the notion that non-caring equals safety has to be unsettled. What needs to be conveyed is the idea that a person can be very caring but still be able to set boundaries, say "no," and assert him- or herself. In fact, those who are more openly caring may be better at avoiding exploitation in that they do not always feel guilty about their previous coldness or aloofness and may find it easier to assert themselves in caring ways. This form of assertiveness has many salutary effects and improves the quality of relating overall.

With a relational approach, sometimes clients' needs come into conflict. For instance, many borderline patients often need more therapy time than they can afford. This is mostly due to the difficulty they have in modulating the overwhelming aggression and anxiety that develops when they are separated from caring figures. Once they have entered therapy, they usually become quickly attached to the therapist, and their dependency needs become ferocious. To help them regulate the feelings that accrue from separations, therapists often employ multiple sessions and even offer a few minutes between sessions to allow clients to make phone or internet contact with them as a way to help manage their feelings. Therapists, as human beings, also have needs and feelings and want down time for themselves, need to get paid and have other clients who need their help. Consequently, they cannot be ubiquitously present like a good-enough early mother would be. Rather than falling back on an austere therapeutic frame of confining interaction to proscribed regular therapy hours at the going rate, therapists may adjust their fees to make more sessions available to the client. They may also allow something like two five-minute phone calls per week outside therapy hours. In this case, therapists have to be cognizant of their needs and feelings and how much they are willing to give to the client. They may need to negotiate, as it were: "I can reduce my fee by one third, but not half. I can allow two five-minute phone calls and no more." The important factor is that the therapist brings her or his real needs into interaction with the client, who as a person gets involved. Clients, with their own subjective needs and wants, may push for something different, but the real needs of the therapist may only allow for so much give, and both parties have to determine if they can embrace the therapeutic endeavor given their particular circumstances and life positions. But two real people are negotiating in this dyad.

Here is another example of bringing the therapist's personhood or subjectivity into the treatment. Jeff came into treatment with anhedonia, low-grade paranoia, difficulty forming a romantic relationship and deadness in his erotic and sexual experience. We had previously worked on his Oedipal anxieties, his fear of aliveness and his fear of intimacy. I had been interpreting how he feared attack if he allowed his sexual feelings to fill his body. All this worked in measure, but he still seemed to be able to experience sexual feelings primarily intellectually. This would register and he would say, "Yes, I do feel a little sexual or stimulated," but then the feelings would quickly disappear by way of repression or disavowal.

Taking a different tack, I decided to bring myself into therapy. Jeff was discussing an attractive woman he saw lecturing on the internet. I asked him to show me the video and then said, "I wouldn't kick her out of bed for eating crackers." Jeff laughed quite a bit. He was not used to another "guy" joining him in this typical way of playing with sexual impulses. At another time, he told me how he had seen a woman's knee appear as she sat across from him folding her legs. He also said she knew he was excited about the view. I said, "I think she liked you looking up her dress." He laughed again and said, "I wasn't looking up her dress." I said, "Oh, too bad. Maybe you missed something." He then laughed more. I do believe the effect this had on Jeff gave him permission, by way of our relationship and self-disclosure, to more strongly embrace and embody his sexual feelings. He has continued to talk more freely about his sexual feelings, has reduced his contempt for women and has begun to elaborate his loneliness and longing for relationship more thoroughly.

Still another example of the use of relationship involves a woman who was agoraphobic. After working with me for many months, she told me that her husband had received pictures from his cousin's Hawaiian vacation. This made the husband furious at his wife because it had been years since they had taken a vacation. She went on for quite a while about how upset he was, how guilty she was and how horrible it is to disappoint her husband in this way. Picking up on the side of her conflict that urgently wanted to change, I felt compelled to say, "Why don't you just take a short day trip somewhere to start the process of eventually going on vacation?" She rather calmly acknowledged the wisdom of such an idea, and we finished the session. Two days later, when she came in for her next session, she was furious with me. "Your stock is going way down. How could you say such a thing?" she asked. "You are just like every other therapist I have ever had who could never help me. Don't you think if I could I would? That's my problem, I can't. I have tried before and I have panic attacks and can't sleep and we have to leave in the middle of the night, if we make it that far." I then realized that I was feeling guilty about not resolving her troubles more quickly. I had felt scared and just exhorted her to change in spite of the fact that she had not done enough therapeutic work to make a trip with her husband a real possibility. At that moment, I said, "I am sorry. I failed you. I got scared about your husband being mad and your disappointment, so I pushed you to change." She retorted, "You went off the reservation." I said, "Yes, I went off the reservation. I forgot myself and, more importantly, I forgot you and your troubles." She eventually went on to say, "Okay, your stock is going back up."

This apology and repair of my mistake had several salutary effects as far as I could see. First, it helped her feel her subjectivity was respected. She is a real person with a position and feelings that need to be heard. Second, she was able to be mad at me and express it and her disappointment without retribution, defensiveness or revenge on my part, which left her feeling I could survive her anger and remain a good object. Third, she did not have to split off her anger so she could sustain ambivalence toward me: both liking me and being mad at me, which is something she has had a hard time doing as she historically had to repress, dissociate or split off her anger from her affectionate feelings. I do not think some of these therapeutic gains could have been achieved had I tried to maintain a position of neutrality and simply made interpretations about the genesis of her anger or her anxiety about being angry with me in the therapy.

That our relationship with others sits squarely at the center of spiritual, emotional and psychological development points us to the ethics and philosophical foundations of the relational/ intersubjective turn in depth psychology. The relational school grew out of the intersection of interpersonal, object relational and self-psychological schools of psychoanalysis. Interpersonal theory, an extension of Harry Stack Sullivan's theory, emphasized the importance of interpersonal interactions with others, while object relations theory—an extension of Winnicott, Fairbairn, Balint, Kernberg and others—emphasized the intrapsychic representation of early relationships in the mind known as *introjects*, which continue to influence the types and quality of all future relationships. Self-psychology, developed by Kohut, emphasized the importance of interactional therapeutic failures on the part of the analyst/therapist and the importance of empathy and emotional presence with the patient.

The confluence and integration of these schools mostly has found its home under the philosophical umbrella of social constructivism, which broadly holds that knowledge is constructed or co-created through the interaction of two people or groups. It deemphasizes even hard biological science, as it, too, is a narrative that can be influenced by current cultural and contextual perspectives. While social constructivism is not the only philosophy that has provided a home to the relational perspective, it is the predominant one. Phenomenological and existential psychologies are also employed as underpinnings for the relational/intersubjective approach.

Interestingly, the relational/intersubjective movement with its emphasis on the realness of the relationship, de-emphasis of transference and counter transference in favor of authentic relating and the deemphasis of unconscious motivation, resembles the earlier existential/humanistic perspectives of Rollo May (2007) and Clark Moustakas (1969). Again, the relationship with empathy, authentic relating and embeddedness in the context of the relational world around us takes center stage.

A fundamental difference between the two schools, however, is the perceived nature of the self. From the phenomenological position of Heidegger, the self-object dichotomy is unsettled and the self spans the dichotomy of "I" and "world." *Dasien* is Heidegger's expression of a self inextricably embedded in life and the world, extending the self beyond the Cartesian isolated mind. Even though the self is basically created by active choice in phenomenological existential theory, there is a self embedded in the world to build on. Free will is then emphasized as an essential element of the self, which the self uses to chart its own destiny.

> The term *Dasein* proposes radically to overcome Cartesian subject/object dualism and by highlighting the perspective that the human individual exists, not as an encapsulated ego, but, rather, as a realm of world openness, a being-in-the-world...when human beings meet, they do not experience each other as separate monads of consciousness, which must then find some way to interact, but, rather they immediately find one another existing out in the world together... (Craig, 2007, pp. 6–7)

Relational psychoanalysis, under the umbrella of social constructivism, unsettles the self in a more radical way by positing the self as a construction of a relational or cultural matrix. The self then becomes a determinant of the relational narrative and lacks what we call an essential quality. The *self as other* or the *self as multivocalties* are often employed as descriptors. The self as a two- person construct is another often used adage. The analytic third is another similar perspective (Ogden 2004). The analytic third is a co- constructed new reality that is developed between analyst and patient/therapist, which allows both to introject a new and better developed experience of self.

These more relational/intersubjective perspectives from either the postmodern or earlier phenomenological points of view are attempts to take us away from the perspective of the person as an isolated mind. This has a great deal of value. They are also attempts to unsettle the analyst/therapist as having a God's eye view of the subjectivity of the other and place the patient back as an active agent in the therapeutic dyad and as one who may have his or her own privileged knowledge of him- or herself. Both the unsettling of the analyst as absolute expert who knows what is right and wrong with the client, and promoting the client as an active participant in the therapeutic dyad have merit for psychoanalytic praxis. In addition, the insertion of the analyst into the therapeutic encounter, with his own needs, wants, fears and desires that can be used as leverage for therapeutic change, also brings important benefits into play. Although therapeutic mistakes are more frequent with the relational approach, the repair of these mistakes by way of empathy, understanding and often apology offers a built-in, powerful therapeutic tool that helps clients and therapists alike feel authentic, genuine and empowered as individuals. The embrace of the complexity of our personhood, including both our higher and lower natures, promotes the actualization of our core possibilities and spiritual potential.

Chapter 4
Core Self Dialogues

Conversations with Rose

What follows is a series of email correspondences between Rose Koenig and me. Rose and I met in Mike Eigen's chat room and have continued an edifying online relationship. As we continued to talk online, I began to feel that the inclusion of some of our conversation in the book would be helpful since she asks many questions that someone getting acquainted with my work might want to ask. Rose's thoughtful questions also provided inspiration for completion of the text. She is professor of literature and a film lecturer at the Academic College of Tel Aviv Yaffo.

Rose: Recently I came across the discussion of this fascinating dream—I think it was in an article by Ferro (1993) but can't be sure—and wanted to run it by you. Patient brings in the following dream: She is walking toward her house with her therapist where they're going to have the session. Therapist is walking a little behind her talking on his phone. She keeps looking back to make sure he's there. He smiles at her and keeps talking on the phone. She gets to the house. Therapist is nowhere to be seen. She tries to find a room for the therapy but can't find any available space. Therapist doesn't show. Suddenly she looks outside and sees snowflakes and is very delighted. That's the end of the dream. Now the therapist when the patient relates the dream is extremely excited about the last part, the patient finding the snowflakes, and emphasizes the upbeat ending and spends little time talking about the beginning and end. He encourages the patient to see how she can find things on her own, how she, in fact, doesn't need the therapist. Ferro sees this as an example of a saturated interpretation, leaving no room for additional, different possibilities—a kind of coercive reading of the text and an obvious running away of the therapist in his reading of the dream as he is absent in the actual dream, confirming the patient's fear of the runaway therapist. Happy to hear what you think.

Franklin: Yeah, I think the therapist wants it to be saturated with positive meaning, to let him or her off the hook. I think it's a flight into the positive. My hunch is that the dream is an expression of the patient's anger at therapeutic distance or rejection of some sort. The snowflakes are a crystallization of the patient's anger into a sort of frozen present. The snowflakes are an offering to the therapist to be forgiven about anger at the distance, and it's also an expression of frozen, reaction-formulated aggression into pretty things.

Rose: Just love your answer, Franklin. You know literature is my area but your interpretation is just a a virtuoso reading of the text. Great. Yes, I agree, the therapist is running. The patient brings the dream as an attempt to reach the therapist, to convey her concern, fear, dread of his absence. And yes, the snow signifies the cold and the fear of hot rage—yes, wonderfully put—into pretty things: the anestheticization of anger, a flight into the positive. Once again, the same problematic phenomenon—the running into something good, cheerful, upbeat as a way of avoiding the darkness, the dread.

Rose: I came across something that Eigen wrote in an early article, "Psychopathy and Individuation," which I think is directly related to our discussion of judicious knowing and inimical effects on the patient. He writes that for Winnicott, "in cases where the patient's infantile omnipotence has been pathologically obstructed and inverted, the responsive analyst in some sense allows himself to be created by the patient's omnipotence in order to allow the proper development and outgrowing." I thought that the responsive analyst here would be in diametric opposition to the judicious one who would label the patient a grandiose self and deflate/shame that self through judicious interpretation. My question is: How, practically speaking, does the therapist allow himself to be created by the patient's omnipotence? How is that done in the therapeutic encounter?

Franklin: I think the therapist springs out of the patient's head by way of idealized phantasies. The patient idealizes the therapist and then identifies with him or her. The patient also imbues the therapist with magical, omnipotent powers of repair and ministration, which allows the unconscious, childlike, narcissistic, omnipotent demands to become conscious, emotionally contained instead of repressed, and finally transformed or worked through to some extent.

Rose: Does this have something to do with the patient's need to have an effect on the therapist, to get him to respond. Is that how she senses her omnipotence in that she can play with him the way the child plays with the transitional object. And is that why a more Freudian, classical analysis fails with certain patients—because the therapist is unresponsive, a blank screen?

Franklin: I think omnipotence spans the two-person field. Omnipotence from the patient's point of view is really a demand for omnipotence that is a sense that the world, others, should totally gratify all needs without delay. If they don't, the omnipotent child–patient becomes angry. The patient correspondingly feels a sense of elevation of the self to sooth the low self-esteem that comes from guilt and shame that the child omnipotence creates in the patient. The patient has no real grounded self-esteem which accrues from being a loving person, tolerating frustration, believing he or she is good and valuable. The patient expects obeisance from others because he or she narcissistically needs all these adorations, ministrations and power to sooth the damaged self-worth which has been fixated in the personality, usually through trauma. The therapist fields all this by way of transference and his or her transference to the patient also gets brought into play. Can the therapist survive the attacks that come from the demand for omnipotence? Can he or she be loving instead of revengeful when the patient attacks? Has the therapist worked through enough of his or her own material to contain and detoxify the hate and demands or does he or she counteract in negative ways? It's a complicated answer. Sorry.

Franklin: Yes, these patients need to be responded to. Some needs have to be gratified. If not, they cannot tolerate the frustration and their anger becomes unbearable and they leave therapy. Freudians used to call these patients unanalyzable. I think it was Kohut who first brought a thoughtful and organized meta psychology and practice into play with these patients.

Rose: Here's a question: If, to simplify, most patients are looking for a healthy bond to replace toxic bonds from the past, why is the therapeutic encounter so fraught with danger, disruption, eruption? Why is it so hard to forge that bond if, in fact, that is the primary goal of therapy, a healthy, resilient, elastic, honest WE that is the key to healing and growth?

Franklin: My answer is, I think, many faceted. They are looking for a positive bond while simultaneously they are not. They don't trust the other, the relationship. They/we project our own hateful feelings such as envy, spite, judgmentalness, revenge and so forth, so that the good in life is not trusted. The good is avoided as it is simultaneously longed for. Love outraged from earlier trauma also turns into hate. Hate causes unconscious guilt, which makes us feel undeserving and afraid of anything good. Trauma also creates angry dependency such that when a therapist or anyone doesn't meet our hungry demands we want to kill them. We feel they are persecuting us by not fulfilling our entitled demands, so we punish the one we love, causing further guilt and paranoia, and a feeling that relationships are not safe unless we are ruthless and controlling. The way out is to see the pain of the early trauma as causing hate. Then we need to contain it, modulate it and detoxify it by caring for ourselves and the other without repressing the hate, which is why we as therapists love it when people own their hate in a self- reflective way. We don't want them to always only identify with niceness. We know they are nice but we want to know their complexity, their lower and base feelings in liberating containment and perhaps self-reflective play. Ha, you got me on a roll,

Rose. Maybe this answer fits; maybe you have some different thoughts.

Rose: Basically what you're describing, Franklin, is the beta to alpha process—digesting the beta and giving it back to the patient in palatable form. But I remember in Eigen's discussion of Bion that the beta serves a purpose in its own right. There is a vitality, aliveness, realness, ferocity, truthfulness, energy in beta. Ferro talks about changing tomatoes into salsa—but maybe tomatoes want to remain tomatoes, don't want to be squished and squashed. Maybe tomatoes want the therapist to be their friend AS THEY ARE, without conversion. Just let them be. Maybe so many of the collisions between patient and therapist arise when the patient senses exactly that, the therapist trying to convert, to change, transform. Very, very tricky.

Franklin: Hi Rose, This is a very late response but I was going through our thread and wanted to respond. I think Ferro's notion that "maybe tomatoes want to stay tomatoes," that maybe tomatoes want the therapist to be their friend AS THEY ARE without conversion strikes at the heart of a complex problem. Bion's beat elements, to the extent that they contain globules of darkness that are unarticulated, call up the notion that they need containment by a friendly figure, a friendly "container," which invites them out of hiding, accepts them and holds them with care. Some of these dark elements contain anti-life qualities, however, such as the desire to punish others or the self, or intentions to be cruel to others. While these elements, or tomatoes, need to be accepted, befriended and not forced to change, they can wreak havoc on a personality. They can destroy a person's self-esteem, cause conscious and unconscious guilt, cause anxiety and paranoia when projected and cause depression when turned on the self. When these beta/tomato elements are accepted or contained as is, they still can wreak havoc as people intrinsically feel bad about these impulses. No amount of superego acceptance alters the fact that these malevolent impulses still create pain and problems when only contained. Containment of beta/tomato elements as they are is very liberating to a point, but transformation, not repression or disavowal, has greater salutary, emancipatory effects, in my opinion. The idea that hate is "love outraged" captures the idea that hate is a response to anti-love experience. If scathing hate can be recognized as a response to severe psychic pain or trauma, one can see that it accrues from the injury and is not a part of us just because we are born bad. The child who longs for love and is neglected, abused, forsaken develops this scathing hate and cruelty, not someone who has had a "facilitating environment."

Most believe that hate and malevolence deserve an equal place in the "guest house" as a result of their being spurned for so long, and I think they are right in many ways. I think they are right in the sense of transitional phenomena, but just act this hate and malevolence out in the world and people get damaged, abused and hurt, in the name of being real. I think containment of dark beta/tomato elements is helpful in this transitional space kind of way, but transformation is a greater calling. This is true, I believe: While many are just stuck in the idea of relegating these elements to the unconscious and living a false self kind of existence and more advanced souls are into accepting things as they are, I think becoming something more, while simultaneously accepting yourself as you are, is ultimately most helpful. It reminds me of the old saying that you have to accept yourself as you are to be what you want to be. I don't think this is Mike's or Bromberg's or Ferro's position, but it is mine. This is a long answer, I know, but I wanted to respond even if it's a month later. P.S. This is what my book's about. Much of the material we discuss, I discuss in the book.

Rose: Thanks, Franklin, for your insights into rage and hate and blackness. I think you're right that we can't just throw tomatoes when we want, but I do think that in the therapeutic encounter we have the unique opportunity to BE all we can't be in the real world outside. And then comes the challenge—if the therapist responds to the blackness, the rage in a judicious or fearful way, if he, too, runs from the grizzly, the panda, then the patient continues to be ashamed of this potentially vital and vitalizing part. I keep going back to that moment Eigen brings up when the rageful patient is about to stomp out the door and Eigen gets up and hugs her and writes that he feels a vitality, energy, life-affirming spirit in her rage. That, for me, is the remarkable moment—to understand that the rage is a defiance against compliance, a stripping away of judiciousness and falseness and civility. It's Bion's freeing murder, Loewald's emancipatory murder, Virginia Woolf's killing of the angel, Arendt's wanting to be more than the sunshine girl. And the irony is that the more we accept this darkness, blackness, the less it needs to rage because it is being seen, recognized. I think of Bertha Mason in Bronte's *Jane Eyre*, locked up in the attic, the madwoman in the attic; I think of what Eigen told someone he was supervising, to cut the patient some slack, not to straighten her out, allow her her madness. There is something about the therapeutic process that seems too judicious, too knowing. Heidegger's response to Arendt's shadow self was disgusting, colonizing. Who is he to say who she is? It's Pygmalion again but in a more invidious fashion. My point is that for many who come to therapy there is a strong need to reveal Hyde so that they can live their lives more freely, with less shame and blame, until the blackness comes into the room. And perhaps the therapist brings his blackness in, as well, the way you did with the dead babies joke— true healing and growth can't take place. That's why that dream with the snowflake that the therapist emphasized and skipped over the darker aspects of the dream was such a resounding failure. Just talk to the tomatoes. Don't try to change them. And just in talking to them, recognizing them, allowing them their fullness and redness, transformation will come. Change comes with acceptance, recognition, validation and sharing, sharing of blackness, darkness, rage, excess, intensity, hate, being "bad" and "mad" together.

Rose: I came across this article by Stolorow, Atwood and Orange (1992) where they discuss among other things the secret love affair between Heidegger and Arendt. What I found particularly fascinating, and this confirms our theory that most people, including analysts, are afraid of the dark, is a passage from Arendt's diary called "Shadows" which she sends to Heidegger, telling him of her darker self, her "double nature." And Heidegger responds, "There are shadows only where there is sun. I would not love you if I were not convinced that those shadows were not you but distortions and illusions." Now I've always hated Heidegger because he was a Nazi sympathizer but when you read his arrogant, judicious colonization of Arendt's mind, he knows what she is and is not. He wants what he calls his "sunshine girl" and refuses to hear, listen, see anyone else. How invalidating, how annihilating. Reminds me of that dream the patient brings in with the snowflake and the therapist is delighted with the snowflake and elides, erases, discards anything dark or dreary or anxiety-inducing in the dream. Well, here we have it again. It's just amazing. EVERYONE loves the sunshine girl; no place for the dark, shadowy self. Hyde always needs to hide—amazing how consistent and pervasive the pattern.

Franklin: What is particularly troublesome from Heidegger is the phrase, "I would not love you if I were convinced that the shadows were not you." While it is important to convey a person is more than their shadow, to say or suggest that someone's dark side renders them unlovable is oppressive. Maybe Heidegger didn't quite mean what he said, but given his exquisite use of language he probably did mean it as it reads. If someone is forced into their sunshine persona and loses the complexity of the darkness or shadow existent within them, they inhabit what Winnicott calls the false self or a mask of goodness that shrouds, disavows, relegates the shadow to otherness, which is very problematic and blocks real containment, integration or transformation. Hyde always needs to hide his shadow. The sunshine girl is forced into a similar conflict with Heidegger's lack of acceptance of Arendt's shadow.

Rose: You're absolutely right. Unfortunately, though, Heidegger is not alone in asking women to remain sunshine girls. It's a gender thing and it drives me crazy. I look at this with my students. We've talked about this before—angel/demon dichotomy. Woolf's killing the angel to lead a fuller, freer life; obviously she didn't do such a good job. Women not allowed to be angry—called castrating bitches. This goes far beyond Heidegger and Arendt. I see it as a serious problem in our society and, unfortunately, in therapy as well, where the therapist frequently wants the sunshine girl, not the raging one. I wonder if again this is a gender thing and the therapist would be more accepting of a male patient's aggression, hostility, rage than a female patient's. For me, the most infuriating part of Heidegger's response was his telling her what she really is, his KNOWING. WTF is that? We're back to the judicious knowing. I don't think there's anything more catastrophic for the therapeutic relationship than that judicious knowing. The irony is that this is perhaps one of the few professions where all the expertise and knowledge you've gained has to be kept hidden, so to speak, and what works best is the feeling that two PEOPLE, not patient and therapist, are sitting in a room sharing, being honest, allowing for anything and everything to enter the room and being PLAYFUL— playfulness between two people, not sick patient, healthy therapist. Bottom line, I would say illusion, restoring illusion in the therapeutic encounter is necessary, crucial, critical. To paraphrase Wilde, too much reality can kill you.

Franklin: I do think Little Miss Sunshine is a feminist issue. Women are not allowed to be angry at life, at kids. They are supposed to JUST be mothers—all good, nothing bad. This element of their personality has to be foreclosed.

   We had a woman here, maybe about 15 years ago, who killed all of her kids. She told her husband, family, friends again and again she couldn't cope with her anger at them. She felt trapped; no one would listen. She asked her husband to not leave her alone with the kids but he did. She finally drove her car into a lake and killed the children. No one would let her have her dark side—respect it and help her with it. She was a mom. Momhood was supposed to totally define her. This happens a lot in smaller ways every day, a million times. It makes me very sad right now, but I usually feel mad about it.

Rose: Can't tell you how happy it makes me that you agree. Horrific story with that woman, but it tragically confirms exactly what you and I say—no room for anyone but Miss Sunshine and then when this woman was crying out for help, she was ignored, depreciated, probably told to pull herself together. Disgusting—they should be held as accomplices to the crime. Yes, something is truly rotten in a society that silences, strangles women, allows only the angel to speak. Angel/demon dichotomy is still alive and well—just frightening.

Rose: This is probably a dumb question showing I'm not in the field no matter how much I read, but I'll ask it anyway: If the repetition compulsion is at the heart of the therapeutic encounter, if the patient tries again and again to rework the trauma via her relationship with the therapist, how, in fact, does it get reworked? The therapist noting to the patient that it is a repetition compulsion does not seem of much help—that's left brain to left brain. What needs to happen between patient and therapist in the here-and-now to make the there-and-then fade, recede, become less haunting, less now and more then?

Franklin: I am always impressed by how much you know about psychoanalysis. Your short question is so foundational and far reaching that it is difficult to answer it. You are right that pointing out the transference as repetition compulsion has little utility. It may help a little in the sense of helping the patient to become more self-reflective about his or her end of an enactment. Pointing out the repetition by way of enactment is left brain to left brain and resembles a classical approach of making the issue conscious. Consciously knowing that an enactment is occurring does little to change it. Most change takes place as unconscious learning—that is, in some way without conscious awareness.

    A client I am treating suffering from obsessions and unmetabolized aggression is always doubting, worrying, and afraid he will act out his "odd" aggressive and sexual impulses. As compensation he is passive and repressed. I absentmindedly fail to notify him that I will not be at a session; he shows up, I don't. This is my second missed session in three years. He is furious and cancels the next session and states he has to mull over whether he should continue therapy with me, as this is the second time I have displayed a callous disregard for him and his needs. He says that I am treating him like dirt and he would never do that to me. My thoughts were that he is experiencing me like his father who treated him like dirt. My lack of conscientious concern had similarities to his paternal rejection, criticism and disregard. I did not interpret the transference. My response was I was sorry; I fucked up. I feel very badly about this. He says, I will not take this, I don't think I will be coming back. I am sure you don't do this to other people. I said, I am very sorry, I really did fuck up, but I really hope you don't get so mad at me that you stop your therapy. That would hurt you. Also, I do do this to other people. I miss sessions sometimes with interns, too. It is my problem. I am both absent minded and work a little too much so I think I let things get by me at times. While this hurts you it is not something I explicitly do to you alone. I know missing two sessions in three years is a problem, but many people would find it forgivable. I hope you do too. He then said you are trying to tell me something here. Okay, I will think about it and see you in two weeks. Two weeks later he came back and said he was not mad me any longer. We talked about it a little more. He then told me that I reminded him of his father who was so callous to him. I said I understood and apologized again.

I didn't interpret the reiteration of an earlier object relationship. I allowed the patient to be angry with me without being defensive or revengeful. I think not blaming the patient for overreacting was important. Apologizing for my wrongdoing was important, and even clarifying that this is an overall problem for me with others and that he is an equal opportunity casualty of my problems was important. The patient was able to review and self-reflect when I was non-defensive and apologetic. Unlike earlier experience I, as the paternal authority, apologized and shared vulnerable aspects of myself that the patient could use to understand my subjectivity and feel me to be an equal person, not a high-and-mighty father. The patient could have his anger in a constructive way, and by sharing my issues he could be angry yet modify and regulate it. My saying I apologize but I hope you will forgive me helped him see me as a subjective person, not simply a hierarchical authority. This, overall, helped repair old wounds, contain and modify affect, perhaps grieve old wounds by connecting his anger at me with his father, organically change a felt sense that all male authorities are mean and that he has only two options—fight or flight—and in addition realize we would both survive his anger. This was a lot to learn. and it all happened without me commenting on these issues or making them conscious by way of interpreting what was happening in his mind.

There are other change factors, such as modification of a harsh superego by way of the patient identifying with and internalizing the therapist's more benevolent attitude. Perhaps idealizing the analyst and internalizing the idealization into the self-representation, or Klein's movement from the paranoid position to a felt awareness of both love and hate for the therapist. Change even happens by reviewing these dynamics in extra-transferential relationships, or the patient's everyday relationships. There are really many ways people change, but how change happens in the therapeutic enactment without simply thinking it is an interpretation is what I outlined above. For a more thorough take on how I think change happens by way of transference and countertransference ups and downs, you could read my 2004 "Mourning, trauma and working through" paper in the Psychoanalytic Review. In fact, I'll send it to you now in case you want to read it. It was written over ten years ago when I was a bit more traditional in my approach. Well, that's a mouthful.

Rose: I reread your article—again, very impressive. Here's my question and it comes up all the time: What is it with mourning that it is considered such a pivotal part of the process? You talk of the "hard pain of her outrage turned to softer pain of grief, shame and sadness." Why can't the outrage and rage be the therapeutic part? Why the emphasis in everything I read on mourning? It reminds me of Klein's valorizing the depressive over Paranoid Schizoid position, and Eigen, in his discussion of Bion, showing the dialectical tension between the two without privileging any one state. Why does the rage have to be softened or transformed? I guess I'm missing something here, or maybe because I come from the world of literature and the Lears and Ahabs whose rage is seen as an heroic capacity to rise above, to defy the gods. Why does the rage have to be transformed into mourning.

Franklin: As to your question, it's always tricky. Why you don't privilege one over the other is because if you do you run the risk of foreclosing the other. If you emphasize the benefits of the depressive position people may run to it, because it is framed as desirable. The same with rage and hate; if you say there is always love within the hate, the fear is people will try to bypass the hate with denial and the use of rational functions. It's not at all wrong to emphasize the negative and positive, you might say, in equal proportion. It is an attempt to live beyond duality, beyond the dichotomy of love and hate. I privilege the outcome a little more of the liberated love, which often comes through a mourning process. I do this with a large dose of caution to always pay attention to your darker side. Pay attention to your hate, your cruelty, your entitlement, your envy and so forth, but don't believe it is the ultimate you. Identify it, but don't identify with it. We are all divine sparks and as such, we are all aspects of benevolent divinity. That's my opinion.

Rose: I thought of what you wrote, Franklin, about us all being divine sparks, and I think of the God of Judaism who rages and avenges. I think of Moses who raged at the rock rather than talking to it—a Moses who was so human and vulnerable and all the more heroic for his trespasses and transgressions. So I think we're all happy with our divine sparks, with our goodness and generosity. But like in that Heidegger and Arendt example where she asked him to see not only the sunshine girl, the divine side of her, but also the dark, shadowy side and he, in all his pompous judiciousness and self-aggrandizement, refused to do so, the therapeutic encounter MUST include a welcoming of the darker self; otherwise it's only a pseudoanalysis—darkness AND light, rage AND mourning, Paranoid Schizoid and Depression positions, no privileging, no valorizing, no judiciousness, no colonizing, no silencing, no relegating, no delegating. What a wonderfully freeing experience that could be.

Franklin: The darker side must always be welcome. I get what you say about identifying with it, too. It is a part of us, filled with life, but so many of my patients when they discover their darkness begin to think it defines them. When they see, feel that they really want to hurt people, sometimes with cruelty, they think since it is under their false self-presentation that the cruelty is who they really are. This belief that the cruelty is who they really are drives them to repress and foreclose again. So I tell them that is not who you ultimately are, this is your love outraged. While you need to look for your shadow, embrace it, this comes from the child within you who was longing for love and was injured badly. I have always found this to be helpful. Heidegger could have said; I love all of you, your dark and your light and the dark contains your light.

Rose: I get what you're saying—I think the patient's ability to freely explore whom they'd like to kill, hurt, strangle is wonderful. Transitional space, potential space is exactly about freeing our "bad" selves, not in real time, but in that room together, the way you did when you had the courage to share with the group your envious, murderous thoughts, feelings. The more we can be in touch, share those thoughts, feelings, the less we have to act out in the real world, in real time. Yes, that pompous know-it-all Heidegger could have said he loved her, light and dark—he could have also admitted that he, too, had a light and dark. They could have even laughed about their darker selves, darker thoughts. But once again that would have meant seeing her not as the sunshine girl, this idealized image of woman, but as a person, a human-being—back to the angel/demon dichotomy. And that's why I think particularly for women in therapy it's important to bring in the shadow self.

Rose: I like that, the dark contains your light— wonderful. Wonder if that's like Bion's beam of darkness, or the darkness that fills us with light. Once read this article, think by Ruth Stein, "The Unbearable Lightness," about a patient who became terribly disoriented, felt lightheaded if he didn't have negative feelings about someone, something—the lightness was unbearable. Needed the angry, the rageful, the hateful to feel grounded, real, alive. Thought that was very interesting.

Franklin: Hate, rage, contempt, negativity can become a habit pattern. People feel ungrounded when they challenge it as a default position.

Musings with Troy

The following is a dialogue between Troy Piwowarski and myself. Troy is an existential phenomenological psychologist who teaches for the Existential Humanistic Integrative training program in San Francisco and maintains a private practice in psychotherapy in Troy, MI.

Troy: I wonder how this perspective of an underlying unity can be reconciled with a more atheistic or open-ended existential perspective of the likes of Yalom or Sartre. The main philosophical departure seems to be the assumption that this life, with all its ambiguity and mystery, ultimately means something, that it all coheres into some ultimate organizing principle, rather than having multiple possibilities of meaning we assign it, or even perhaps being chaos, as some of the more absurdist existentialists suggest. Does it seem possible to maintain the basic openness of this particular existentialism, while also holding to this assumption of an underlying unity to everything?

Franklin: This is a complex question. It has at least two parts. In some ways my perspective can be reconciled with theirs and in some ways it can't. Phenomenology is an easier fit than existentialism. Phenomenology unsettles the subject–object distinction, which is very congruent with the core self that has a simultaneous dual union or self–other identity.

If one takes what might be characterized as a hard existential position, consciousness absolutely ends with death—no ifs, ands or buts. Then the world seems absurd in that we are thrown into a meaningless existence, and all we have left is the ability to make meaning in spite of the absurdity. However, if one takes what might be characterized as a softer existential position, that is we are not absolutely sure what happens after we die but we all have to deal with existential angst and finitude because we can't be sure, then this text could work quite well as one approach to make sense of this existential angst. Spirituality can be seen as an existential issue, not simply a maladaptive response. Existentialists such as Kierkegaard and Dostoyevsky could be read this way.

From my perspective there is meaning. Life is not simply chaotic and absurd. Chaos and absurdity reign in the world of duality, which brings conflict and strife. This is the world we mostly see and the one Yalom and Sartre believed totally defines existence. As intrapsychic conflicts—conflicts in the world of duality, conflicts between us and others and life—resolve until the world is experienced by us as more peaceful inside and out, then war outside captures us less. We see it as an evil that is an outpicturing of our world's state of consciousness, which we can affect in benevolent ways with our personal transformation and our being in service of others transformation.

There are still multiple personal possibilities that can be claimed, explored and liberated. Free will still is an essential element of who we are, as Sartre conveyed. However, there is meaning ultimately, even if we cannot apprehend it. "Man is not the measure of all things."

Furthermore, while meaninglessness and absurdity have been privileged in much of the discourse on existentialism, there are some authors who have a more inherent fit. Those existentialists who have more congruence with the position I advocate would be Buber and Levinas, who find meaning, sacredness and divinity in the human encounter and the face of the other. The existential encounter in relationship propels us toward the ineffable, the scared and the divine. Even Victor Frankl finds meaning in the transcendence of the self in love for the other. Love is transcendent and meaningful for Frankl. This is beyond what we create. It is inherent in the fabric of existence.

Troy: The notion of anger, aggression, and basic evil are framed as love outraged in your formulation. There is another perspective from writers like Freud and May that sees aggression and evil as more base than that, harking back to our animal roots. What makes you convinced that aggression is love outraged, and not a more primary human drive all of its own?

Franklin: There is a fundamental positive aggression in the human personality, no doubt. We need to aggress to get food, to find a mate, to take care of ourselves and so forth, and we may need aggression when danger approaches. My point of departure is that cruelty and malevolence are not hard wired in the human personality. In every case I have seen, they come from trauma and at times biological compromise. What I mean by biological compromise is congenital troubles such as an addicted mother who gives birth to a child. Other examples of biological compromise might be alcohol abuse in vitro and perhaps even a history of things such as a mood disorder in the family tree that causes an early temperament up-regulation and vulnerability to injury by anything less than ideal parenting. Biological compromise and early trauma have always been apparent when people develop cruel impulses that cannot be contained. I have not seen it otherwise. Freud's original dual-instinct theory was more in line with this perspective. There were self-preservative instincts and libidinal instincts, and cruelty was a defense against love. Later as he became sick with cancer, patients seemed stuck in their illnesses, and war fell upon him, he became more pessimistic about human nature.

Rollo May, in his famous letters to Carl Rogers, made his case for the "daimonic" in the human personality. He believed this was an innate potential. Of course it is a potential, but again in my clinical history I have always experienced evil related to love outraged. I do think there is one life force, and that is expressed in multiple directions or vectors. Perhaps two basic vectors are love and aggression, but ultimately aggression is in the service of love and self-care until it gets permutated into hostility, vengeance, and meanness and so on.

Troy: As an existential-phenomenological therapist, I have been trained to bracket my own preconceptions and theories about the nature of my patient's inner experience. How do you suggest the neophyte therapist incorporate both the analytic and spiritual aspects of your work, without treading on the patient's unique experience?

Franklin: One should always approach the therapeutic encounter with a "beginners mind." We need to see our clients in fresh and new ways in each session. Everyone, of course, has free will, and also unique personal proclivities, inner strengths, weaknesses and talents. This should always be kept in mind even if all have the basic personality elements of false self, subpersonalities, lower and higher selves. These personality elements are not meant to confine a person's unique personal idiom but rather provide a framework for understanding and transformation. Anytime we assert something, especially with personality theory, we make distinctions that we hope are useful, but I always keep in mind the individual's unique personhood.

Paradoxically, in treatment, or our own self-examination, there is the person that needs to be experienced as fresh, new, authentic; however, there is always the human potential in each of us waiting to be liberated from the shroud of our defenses, negativity, and false- self presentations. The core self is an optimistic personality theory, but anyone who practices in ways that are encouraged by this text should be careful not to use the approach as a template that becomes Max Weber's"iron cage" instead of a door to liberation.

Questions from Lisa
Lisa Kaffenberger recently completed graduate school in psychology and volunteered to pose some questions that she thought might be of interest to new therapists. She practices psychotherapy near South Haven, MI.

Lisa: I would like to understand what "O" is a little more thoroughly. Could you write a little more about it to illuminate me and your other readers?

Franklin: I will try to elaborate some of these difficult concepts a little more, in a sort of Spark's notes kind of way. Understanding Bion is more of a journey than a destination, here are some more thoughts to get started. Bion often uses capital letters such as "O, K, F" and "T," to name a few, as a sort of shorthand note to his thinking. "O" is Wilfred

Bion's conception of an ultimate reality that is beyond thinking and perception. O for the most part contains proto elements of thought that have not been formulated into concise, usable concepts. These proto emotional/thought elements are what he calls beta elements. When these beta elements are contained by a thinker and can be clarified enough to be used by someone to organize experience, they become alpha elements, which can be used to transform and transcend intolerably confusing dualistic and conflictual experience. "K in O" is shorthand for knowledge of O. "T in O" is usually transformations in O, which happen through reverie, communication and faith. Faith for Bion is denoted as "F in O," and equivalent to the analytic attitude. Faith, or F in O, requires patience and acceptance of not knowing and not pushing, truncating, and forcing experience into something already known.

In all, combining Bion's O with something akin to Jung's Transcendent Function suggests a trope in psychological experience toward integration and complexity that is "beyond the iron cage of reason," which many consider mystical liberation.

Lisa: If you are experiencing "love outraged," what "self" is being exposed. And does love outraged always stem from parental/guardianship relationships or is it just from early life experiences?

Franklin: Love outraged stems from early trauma or psychic insult too difficult to bear for the developing infant, toddler or child. Early in life when the child does not have the intellectual or observing capacities to manage parental neglect, abuse, iron fistedness, insults to their subjectivity, the longing for love that stems from the core self is wounded. The little one then feels outraged but usually can do nothing with the outrage since the parents who are committing the abuse and neglect are the same ones who don't care to field the complaint from the child or its anger. These same parents just want the child to behave and be a good boy or girl and comply. Trouble is that the love outraged then goes underground and causes hate, envy, spite, revenge and so forth, which is harder than the original primal anger the child experienced from the neglect or abuse. This tragedy can often be complicated by a biologically sensitive temperament in which the child inherently has a harder time regulating its pain response or reactivity to psychic blows. But love outraged in any case is always organized around the psychic injury.

Let me give you an example. My grandson David, who was two years old at the time, approached his aunt Dee Dee who had just gotten back from vacation and was working on the computer. Dee Dee and David adored each other. When Dee Dee didn't pay much attention to him, he hit her on the head. Aunt Dee Dee was very hurt by this and became angry with the child. She was about to yell at him, and I intervened, asking, "David, are you mad at Dee Dee?" He said, "Yes." I said, "She has been gone a while; did that hurt and make you angry?" He said, "Yes, and she wasn't talking to me." I said, "So you are mad cause she has been gone and not paying attention to you." He then became sad and tearful. When Dee Dee experienced this she opened up her heart again to him and hugged him while David cried and soon felt better. This is a much different approach than just being mad at a child for misbehaving, saying that he is bad and expecting him to just be a good boy. In this scenario his love outraged was acknowledged, his injury was acknowledged, and he did not make abject this wound and its sequelae—love outraged.

Traumata other than the parenting relationship and biological sensitivity can also cause love outraged. Oppressive institutional trauma such as poor daycare, oppressive educational settings, sexual and physical abuse outside the family, racism, physical illness, war, parental illness, extreme poverty, to name a few, can all factor into love outraged. The earlier and more profound the trauma, the more it affects resiliency and all subsequent trauma.

Lisa: What does a person who has gone through the process of liberation look like? Is it an ongoing process that continues forever, or does a person actually reach the best version of his or her core self?

Franklin: It is an ongoing process. We get closer and closer the more work we do and the more resilient we are. On the whole, as one approaches a more thorough liberation of the core self, problems don't cease but they become more manageable and in a funny sense less problematic. Problems are seen more as stepping stones to further liberation rather than injurious events with no relation to the self. Fear, worry and anxiety are seen as faults to be worked with and information as to how we are separated from the peace of the core self. Empathy with others and our world around us becomes more apparent and ecological stewardship more common. Liberated people know their dark, lower self side and their false selves quite well and challenge them when they come into play in their lives. I want to caution again that problems do occur. I have met no one in this life who is perfect, but I have met some more creative, joyful and compassionate people who, I believe, live more from the liberated position than others and make it a task, in this life, to self-examine and grow all the days of their existence.

Chapter 5
Self-Analysis and the Liberation
of the Core Self

While it is important to affirm that this spiritual path is best undertaken with the help of a teacher, therapist or analyst, there is also a function of self-analysis. In the end, our spiritual development is our responsibility. As we move along on our spiritual paths, we attract to us more and more appropriate helpers. Each step of the way, as we progress, different teachers or helpers will evidence themselves in our lives. From the psychoanalytic perspective, this is explained by the notion that because of our psychological defenses, we are only prepared to relate to psychotherapists with a certain degree of training and expertise; otherwise we would feel that therapy is too frightening to us. As we progress, our psychotherapists usually become more and more advanced themselves, as we unconsciously are more ready.

From the spiritual point of view, the axiom that is often espoused is simply, "When the pupil is ready, the teacher will appear." This is very true, but there are times in our spiritual development when we are without a helper, and there are times when we need to be without a helper. It is for these times, when by necessity we are doing our own self-work, that I suggest some techniques for self-analysis. These techniques, ironically, can best be described as psychoanalytic meditations that are designed to facilitate self-analysis. If you are a psychotherapist, you also may teach these to your clients.

First Meditation

Developing the technique of free association as a meditation. In a reclining position, or sitting straight up with your back erect but not stiff, try to relax your mind. After a few minutes, concentrate on your breathing. As you breathe in, gather your tension and as you breathe out, expel your tension with each exhalation. As you do this, you will become more and more relaxed. After this breathing exercise is done, let yourself relax even further for a few minutes and then concentrate on your thoughts. You will "see" all kinds of thoughts floating by, some trivial, some important, some you do not want to acknowledge because they make you emotionally uncomfortable and challenge some cherished idea you may have about yourself. The more uncomfortable thoughts will be, so to speak, mostly in the back of your mind. As you watch the thoughts go by, begin to recognize the thoughts in the back of your mind and begin to try to bring them to the front of your mind. Make a note of them in your mind.

After you do this for five or ten minutes, write them down in black and white or simply record them in your consciousness. Ask yourself then, "What am I afraid of? What feelings do these thoughts evoke? Do I feel I need to stiffen or harden myself against them?" After you can feel that you make a sort of hardened defense against them, tell yourself, "Everything in life and my mind and soul is ultimately benign. Everything in life is ultimately good and constructive. If I am in error, I want to know this and understand how these temporary bad feelings have an ultimate benign grounding in the truth and knowledge that everything that is not immediately benign is love outraged." Trace your outraged love back to the hurt that causes you to turn away from your benign and loving core. As you do this time after time, you will begin to understand and begin to feel liberation from the hold these scary thoughts and defenses have on you. As you proceed daily or intermittently with this mediation, you will feel more and more liberated from your negativity and lower self. You will feel more and more in touch and grounded in your loving spiritual self, and you will feel more lived through by love than controlled by and at the mercy of your pain, fears and negativity.

Second Meditation

Trace your faults back to core self impulses. As in the last meditation, take either a reclining or a seated position with your posture comfortably erect. Again, begin to focus on your breath. As you breathe in, gather all your tension in your breath. As you breathe out, expel your tension and anxiety with each succeeding breath. After a time, begin to allow into your mind any spontaneously negative impulse, trait or feeling that should begin to emerge. As you do this, try to relax and not tense up against the feelings and harden or numb yourself to them. After a time, write these negative feelings, thoughts, impulses or traits down on paper. If you are not prepared to write them down because of resistance or lack of pencil and paper, just record them in your conscious mind.

After they are recorded, one by one compare these negative thoughts and feelings to their benign counterparts that exist beneath the negative feelings and thoughts. For instance, you may feel a sense of envy because you do not have as much as a family member. You may feel happy at one of his or her failures. As you note this, try to see what spiritual self-attitude this envious feeling is a distortion of. Envy, in this case, may hide your own desire to be successful and the impulse to work hard to become successful. You may feel you have the desire but do not want to pay the price of hard work to achieve your goals. After noting this, you may feel more in touch with your desire to pay the price to achieve. If resistance still remains, you can examine what other fear may contribute to holding you back. Perhaps another impulse may be to have sex with someone other than your partner, whom you feel committed to. If you examine this, you may notice the person you fantasize about is someone who you feel to be free-spirited and carefree, unlike your partner. After noting that, you may connect with how you oppressed your partner's desire to be sexy and alive out of fear. This can inform you that you have an erotic sense of adventure that you are afraid of and try to keep under wraps by oppressing your partner. You may then decide to embrace your sense of adventure more courageously rather than giving in to your fear. Here, your more spiritual, vital and loving values of sexuality, adventure and courage that underlie your fears may need to be embraced. Under and within any negative feeling and attitude is the benign, loving impulse gone awry.

Third Meditation

Follow your anxiety to understand your fears. In this meditation, begin as you did in the first two meditations. However, this time as you relax allow yourself to connect with those feelings or thoughts that specifically make you uncomfortable. In this case, you are following the anxiety so that you can find what specifically is bothering you. As you recognize that you are uncomfortable and follow the anxiety, you may become aware of more specific fears. For example: an anxiety about grades in your class may reveal a sense that you are afraid you are inherently inferior to others. You may think that your entire well-being rests with thinking that somehow you are a superior student "thinker" than the next person. As you examine this in the light of day, as it were, you can reassure yourself that your value does not come from being the best student. In fact, some good students can be very depressed and unhappy. Your value comes from how kind and emotionally generous you can be with yourself and others. This, then, helps ground you and dissipates your fears that are based on academic competition and inadequacies. Any fault that underlies anxiety can be examined in this way. Any fault, when examined, reveals a distorted need and wish that comes from the spiritual self and the unitive state that has been distorted. When examined and worked with, these anxieties, which reveal faults and fears, can be challenged and peace begins to emerge as an alternative to anxiety.

Fourth Meditation

Examine the tension in your body to encourage self-transformation. Take either position suggested in the previous meditations. As you breathe and relax, let yourself feel which parts of your body are tense and holding or numb. The tension and holding or numbness, if breathed into in a relaxed way, can reveal insights into our unconscious selves. As you breathe into the tension, allow yourself to associate with the tension or numbness. What comes to mind? Are your hands straining with a desire to reach out to someone? Is your back tense? Do associations come to mind that suggest you want to get your back into something? For example, perhaps you want to push and force because you do not trust the benevolence of life. Maybe you feel if you do not push others and make a specific career opportunity happen, or a certain amount of income happen, you will be shamed. This, then, can be examined against the law of brotherhood and sisterhood, which suggests we are all in this together and do not need "x" amount of income to be valued by others—at least others that matter to be valued by. We need enough income to take care of our needs, not enough income to triumph over others.

A tension in our groin may reveal a genital longing we may have previously failed to recognize. A tension in our mouth may reveal a desire to reach out and suck or take in something or someone else. All these feelings, needs and longings have benevolent and loving impulses at their base. Love is the ultimate reality; that everything else is an illusion must always be kept in mind.

Fifth Mediation

Transforming duality. As you wake up each morning, set the intention to transform duality. Try to take each trouble as it comes. If problems arise, try to breathe into them, relax into them and see if you can take them with a measure of equanimity. It will not be easy, but it can be done. Be careful not to pretend you do not care. Rather, just feel that you care and are fearful, and see if you can let the fear go for moments at a time. If you can let go for moments at a time, you will be able to string such moments together. You will also see, over time, a reduction in the intensity of your fear when something troubling happens. I am not suggesting you will not be sad or have some pain, but those are different feelings than bitterness, spite, depression and so forth. Try this each day and when problems emerge on the horizon. You will see changes over time.

Sixth Meditation

Finding the lesson in problems. As problems arise in your life, instead of raging at life for the problems and at how unfair life is, see if you can turn this around and ask yourself, "What lesson is life trying to teach me?" What have you done to help create this problem, even if it means looking deeply into yourself and finding faults? Although you will feel dysphoric feelings, try not to amplify them, but calmly self-examine and try to see what you need to do to fashion a better life in the future.

If nothing can be done to remedy the situation or trouble you are in at the moment, how can you best handle your situation with grace and dignity? Understanding that life brings pain to everyone at times, what can you do to make the best out of your bad situation?

Seventh Meditation

Using moments of judgment for self-examination. Use moments in your life, when you are unduly tense or judgmental or hyper-invested in an issue to self-examine. It is a version of *looking at the man in the mirror.* When you feel too tense about an event or an interpersonal issue, register it in your mind. After the event has past, ask yourself what fault of yours may be involved. Were you hooked because of your own narcissism, competitiveness, envy, avarice, demandingness or any other character fault? Ask yourself, "What can I do differently next time?" If you were aware of your fault, could you react differently?

For example, once I was very annoyed with a friend who seemed to always need to be right and lord his knowledge over everyone else. I knew he was annoying, but I realized later that I was annoyed beyond what I felt was in measure to the issue at hand. When I examined myself, I realized that I was annoyed with his "know-it-allness" because of my own. I wanted to be the one who knew the most and was on top of the debate or question at hand. After I examined further, I realized that this was how I achieved a lot of my narcissistic gratification. I then realized I did not need to be so angry at something that was also a fault in me. I could even laugh a little at myself.

All these meditations are designed to free you of your layers of defenses and negative feelings and impulses, which cover your spiritual, higher and divine self. I pray they, and any other creative endeavor you can muster, help you on your spiritual path and lead you to greater and greater degrees of guidance and spiritual liberation.

The Steep and Narrow Path

The power within us is rich, complex, loving, unitive, fearless and divine. This power also has personality: individual identity paradoxically intermixed with surrender to universal identity. This power is the core self. Its liberation is the project I advocate. I hope, in some small way, that it helps in your liberation from the shrouds of your own character faults, negativity and fear, which occlude what is fantastic, wonderful and ineffable within you.

I have attempted to take a serious approach to the liberation of the core self, one that avoids, as much as possible, a spiritual bypassing that is, at best, in service of an aggrandized ego element of ourselves. Hopefully, this will help those who want a serious depth approach to their development. It may be a steep and narrow path, but the steep and narrow path is the most true and fruitful in the long run. There are many paths to the top of the mountain or to the depths of our soul. I hope the liberation of the core self will help you on your path.

References

Aron, L. (1996). *A meeting of the minds: Mutuality in psychoanalysis.* Hillsdale, NJ: Analytic Press.

Assagioli, R. (2000). *Psychosynthesis: A manual of principles and techniques.* New York, NY: Hobbs, Dorman. (Original work published in 1965.)

Atwood, G. E., & Stolorow, R. D. (1984). *Structures of subjectivity: Explorations in psychoanalytic phenomenology and contextualism.* New York, NY: Routledge.

Balint, M. (1992). *The basic fault: Therapeutic aspects of regression,* Evanston, IL: Northwestern University Press. (Original work published in 1968)

Banai, E., Mikulincer, M., & Shaver, P. R. (2005). Self object needs in Kohut's self-psychology: Links with attachment, self-cohesion, affect regulation, and adjustment. *Psychoanalytic Psychology, 22*(2), 224–260. doi:10.1037/0736-9735.22.2.224

Beck, A. (1979). *Cognitive therapy and the emotional disorders.* New York, NY: Meridian.

Bion, W. R. (1963). *Learning from experience.* New York, NY: Basic Books.

Bion, W. R. (1965). *Transformations: Change from learning to growth.* London: Tavistock.

Bion, W. R. (1970). *Attention and interpretation: A scientific approach to insight in psycho-analysis and groups.* New York, NY: Basic Books.

Bion, W. R. (2004). *Experiences in groups and other papers,* New York, NY: Routledge. (Original work published 1959)

Binswanger, L. (1963). *Being-in-the world: Selected papers of Ludwig Binswanger* (J. Needleman, Trans.). New York, NY: Basic Books.

Bollas, C. (1989). *Forces of destiny: Psychoanalysis and human idiom.* London: Free Association Books.

Boss, M. (1963). *Psychoanalysis and Daseinanalysis* (L.B.Lefebre,

Trans.). New York, NY: Basic Books. (Original work published in 1957).

Boss, M. (1979) *Existential foundations of medicine and psychology.* New York, NY: Jason Aronson.

Bromberg, P.M. (1996). Standing in spaces: The multiplicity of self and the psychoanalytic relationship. *Contemporary Psychoanalysis, 32*, 509–535.

Buber, M. (1996). *I and thou* (Trans. W. Kaufmann). New York, NY: Touchstone. (Original Work Published 1923)

Bugental, J. F. T. (1965). *The search for authenticity: An existential-analytic approach to psychotherapy.* New York, NY: Holt, Rinehart and Winston.

Bugental, J. F. T. (1976). *The search for existential identity: Patient-therapist dialogues in humanistic psychotherapy.* San Francisco, CA: Jossey-Bass.

Casement, P. (1982). Some pressures on the analyst for physical contact during the re-living of an early trauma. *International. Review of Psychoanalysis*, 9, 279–286.

Cicero, M. T. (1877). *Cicero's Tusculan disputations: also treatises On the nature of the gods, and On the commonwealth* (C.D. Yonge, Trans.). New York, NY: Harper.

Craig, E. (2008). The human and the hidden: Existential wonderings about depth, soul, and the unconscious. *The Humanistic Psychologist, 36*, 227–282.

Davies, J.M. (1998). Multiple perspectives on Multiplicity. *Psychoanalytic Dialogues, 8*, 195–206.

Dorsey, J.M. (1971). *Psychology of emotion: Self discipline by conscious emotional continence.* Detroit, MI: Center for Health Education.

Eigen, M. (1983) Dual union or undifferentiation? A critique of Marion Milner's view of the sense of psychic creativeness. *International Review of Psychoanalysis,* 10, 415–428.

Eigen, M. (1995). *Reshaping the self: Reflections on renewal through psychotherapy.* London: Karnac.

Eigen, M. (1998). *The psychoanalytic mystic.* London: Free Association Books.

Eigen, M. (2004a). *Psychic deadness*. London: Karnac.

Eigen, M. (2004b). *The psychotic core*. London: Karnac.

Eigen, M. (2004c). The sensitive self. Middletown, CT: Wesleyan University Press.

Eigen, M. (2013). *The Kabala and psychoanalysis*. London: Karnac.

Ellis, A. (2004). *Rational emotive behavior therapy: It works for me—It could work for you*. New York, NY: Prometheus Books.

Erickson, E. (1982). *The life cycle completed*. New York NY: Norton.

Erickson, M., Rossi, E., & Rossi, S. (1976). *Hypnotic realities: The induction of clinical hypnosis and forms of indirect suggestion*. New York, NY: Irvington Publishers.

Fairbairn, W.D. (1994). *Psychoanalytic studies of personality*. London: Tavistock Publications Limited. (Original work published in 1952.)

Freud, A. (1923). The relation of beating phantasies to a day dream. *International Journal of Psychoanalysis, 4*, 89–102.

Freud, S. (1915). Instincts and their vicissitudes. In J. Strachey (Ed. & Trans.), *The standard edition of the complete works of Sigmund Freud* (Vol. 14, pp. 117–140). London: Hogarth Press.

Freud, S. (1924). The economic problem of masochism. In J. Strachey (Ed. & Trans.), *The standard edition of the complete works of Sigmund Freud* (Vol. 19, pp. 155–170). London: Hogarth Press.

Gargiulo, G. J. (2004). *Psyche, self and soul: Rethinking psychoanalysis, the self, and spirituality*. London: Whurr Publishers.

Ghent, E. (2002). Wish, need, drive: Motive in the light of dynamic systems theory and Edelman's selectionist theory. *Psychoanalytic Dialogues, 12*, 763–808.

Greenberg, J. R., & Mitchell, S. A. (1983). *Object relations in psychoanalytic theory*. Cambridge, MA: Harvard University Press.

Greenberg , J.R. (1991). *Oedipus and beyond: A clinical theory*. Cambridge, MA: Harvard.

Grotstein, J.S. (1979a). Who is the dreamer who dreams the dream and who is the dreamer who understands it. *Contemporary*

Psychoanalysis, 15, 110–169.

Grotstein, J.S. (1979b) Demonical possession, splitting, and the torment of joy: A psychoanalytical inquiry into the negative therapeutic reaction, unanalyzability and psychotic states. *Contemporary Psychoanalysis, 15,* 407–445.

Grotstein, J. (Ed.). (1981). *Do I dare disturb the universe? A memorial to Wilfred R. Bion.* Beverly Hills, CA: Caesura Press.

Grotstein, J.S. (1998). The numinous and immanent nature of the psychoanalytic subject. *Journal of Analytical Psychology, 43,* 41–68.

Grotstein, J. S. (2000a). *Who is the dreamer who dreams the dream? A study of psychic presences.* Hillsdale, NJ: Analytic Press.

Grotstein, J. S. (2000b). Some considerations of hate and a reconsideration of the death instinct. *Psychoanalytic Inquiry, 20,* 462–280. doi:10.1080/07351692009348900

Hartmann, H. (1954) *Ego psychology and the problem of adaptation.* New York, NY: International Universities Press. (Original work published in 1939.)

Horney, K. (1945). *Our inner conflicts, a constructive theory of neurosis.* New York, NY: W. W. Norton.

Horney, K. (1950). *Neurosis and human growth: The struggle toward self-realization.* New York, NY: Norton.

Husserl, E. (1970). *The crisis of European sciences and transcendental phenomenology* (Trans. David Carr). Evanston, IL: Northwestern University Press. (Original work published 1954)

Huxley, A. (1970). *Perennial philosophy.* New York, NY: Harper & Row.

James, W. (2008). *The varieties of religious experience: A study in human nature.* Waiheke Island: Floating Press. (Original work published in 1902.)

Jung, C. G. (1959). *The archetypes and the collective unconscious.* New York, NY: Pantheon Books.

Jung, C. G. (1951). *Aion: Researches into the phenomenology of the self* (Collected Works Vol. 9 Part 2). Princeton, NJ: Bollingen.

Jung, C. G. (1968). *Psychology and alchemy* (R.F.C. Hull, Trans.) In
    H.Read et al. (series Eds.), The collected works of C.G. Jung
    (Vol. 12.). Princeton, NJ: Princeton University Press. (Original
    work published 1953)

Klein, M. (1975). *Envy and Gratitude and Other Works 1946–1963* (M.
    Masud R. Khan, Ed.). The International Psycho-Analytical
    Library, 104. 1-346. London: The Hogarth Press and the
    Institute of Psycho-Analysis.

Kohut, H. (1971). *The analysis of the self: A systematic approach to the
    psychoanalytic treatment of narcissistic personality disorders.*
    New York, NY: International Universities Press.

Kohut, H. (1977). *The restoration of the self.* New York, NY:
    International Universities Press.

Kohut, H. (1984). *How does analysis cure?* Chicago, IL: University of
    Chicago Press.

Krystal, H. (1985). Trauma and the stimulus barrier. *Psychoanalytic
    Inquiry, 5,* 131–161. doi:10.1080/07351698509533579

Krystal, H., & Krystal, J.H. (1988). *Integration and self healing:
    Affect—trauma—alexithymia.* Hillsdale, NJ: Analytic Press.

Laing, R.D. (1962). *The self and others: Further studies in sanity and
    madness.* Chicago, IL: Quadrangle.

Laing, R.D. (1967). *The politics of experience.* New York, NY:
    Pantheon.

Levinas, E. (1985). *Ethics and infinity.* Pittsburgh, PA: Duquesne
    University Press.

Lewis, C. S. (1955). *Surprised by joy: The shape of my early life.* New
    York, NY: Harcourt.

Maslow, A.H. (1954). *Motivation and personality.* New York, NY:
    Harper.

Maslow, A. H. (1968). *Toward a psychology of being.* New York, NY:
    Van Nostrand Reinhold.

Masters, R. A. (2010). *Spiritual bypassing: When spirituality
    disconnects us from what really matters.* Berkeley, CA: North
    Atlantic Books.

May, R. (1969). *Love and will.* New York, NY: Norton.

May, R. (1975). *The courage to create.* New York, NY: Norton.

Merkur, D. (1999). *Mystical moments and unitive thinking*. Albany, NY: State University of New York Press.

Milner, M. B. (2011). *A life of one's own*. New York, NY: Routledge. (Original work published in 1934)

Lao Tzu (1988). Tao Te Ching (S. Mitchell, Trans.). New York, NY: Harper Collins.

Mitchell, S. A. (1988). *Relational concepts in psychoanalysis: An integration*. Cambridge, MA: Harvard University Press.

Mitchell, S.A. (1991). Wishes, needs and interpersonal negotiations. *Psychoanalytic Inquiry, 11*, 147–170.

Moustakas, C. (1968) *Individuality and encounter: A brief journey into loneliness and sensitivity groups*. Cambridge, MA. Doyle.

Pierrakos, E. (2012). *Complete lectures of the pathwork*. (1996 ed., Vol. 1). Madison, VA: Pathwork Press.

Plotinus (1962). *Plotinus: Selections from his major writings* (A. H. Armstrong, Trans.). New York, NY: Collier Books.

Rank, O. (1945). *Will therapy and truth and reality*. New York, NY: A. Knopf.

Rank, O. (1973). *The trauma of birth*. New York, NY: Harper & Row. (Original work published in 1924.)

Rank, O. (1989). *Art and artist: Creative urge and personality development*. New York, NY: W.W. Norton & Co.

Rogers, C. R. (1961). *On becoming a person: A therapist's view of psychotherapy*. Boston, MA: Houghton.

Rubin, J. B. (1999). *A psychoanalysis for our time: Exploring the blindness of the seeing eye*. New York, NY: New York Universities Press.

Sollars, F.R. (2004). Mourning, trauma and working through. *Psychoanalytic Review, 91*, 201–219.

Sollars, F. R. (2013). A further elaboration of needs in psychoanalysis: Needs in conflict, compromise, and harmony. *Psychoanalytic Review, 100*, 217–237.

Sollars, F. R. (2014). The core self in psychoanalytic literature and its benign and ideal dimensions. *International Journal of Behavioral Research & Psychology, 2*(4), 40–46. doi: 10.19070/2332-3000-140008.

Stolorow, R.D. (2013). Intersubjective systems theory: A phenomenological contextualistic psychoanalytic perspective. *Psychoanalytic Dialogues, 23*(4), 383–389.

Stolorow, R.D. (2014). Undergoing the situation: Emotional dwelling is more than empathic understanding. *International Journal of Psychoanalytic Self Psychology*, 9, 80–83.

Stolorow, R. D., & Atwood, G. E. (1992). *Contexts of being: The intersubjective foundations of psychological life*. Hillsdale, NJ: The Analytic Press.

Stolorow, R.D., Atwood, G.E., & Orange, D.M. (1992). *Worlds of experience: Interweaving philosophical and clinical dimensions in psychoanalysis*. New York, NY: Basic Books.

Sullivan, H. S. (1953). *The interpersonal theory of psychiatry*. New York, NY: Norton.

Underhill, E. (1911). *Mysticism: A study in the nature and development of spiritual consciousness*. Grand Rapids, MI: Christian Classics Ethereal Library.

Valle, R.S. & Steen, H. (Eds.) (1989*). Existential-phenomenological perspectives in psychology*. New York, NY: Plenium Press.

Wainwright, W. J. (2007). *The Oxford handbook of philosophy of religion*. Oxford: Oxford University Press.

Wellwood, J. (1984). Principles of inner work: Psychological and spiritual. *The Journal of Transpersonal Psychology, 16*, 63–73.

Winnicott, D. W. (1965a). *The family and individual development*. London: Tavistock.

Winnicott, D. W. (1965b). *The maturational processes and the facilitating environment*. New York, NY: International Universities Press.

Winnicott, D. W. (1971) *Playing with reality*. New York, NY: Basic Books.

Glossary

Atman: The Hindu core self that expresses a Distinction Union paradox.

Affective Resonance: A person's ability to resonate and experience the same affect in response to viewing a display of that affect by another person.

Affect Tolerance: The ability to affirm and maintain a positive mood as one brings up fears of being swept away or of losing oneself.

Affirming the Existence of the Core Self: The therapeutic process of recognizing that each person has a core self with loving qualities that can make tolerable the negative transference and affective states that seem otherwise unbearable.

Angry Dependency: Accrues from a neglectful or rejecting parental environment in which a person grows up feeling he or she must always receive gratification of needs for caring, esteem, and narcissistic valuing way beyond healthy proportions, thus crippling his or her own needs for independence, autonomy and self-agency.

Anhedonia: Either an avoidance of or inability to experience pleasure.

Arrogance and Vanity: Exaggerated and excessive sense of one's own importance, achievements and abilities that is an attempt to rise above others as a way to resolve feelings of inferiority.

Assagioli's Psychosynthesis Model: A theory that the lower unconscious is split off from what Assagioli calls the higher self and fragmented into subpersonalities.

Basic Rule of Psychoanalysis: Liberation of the core employs the basic rule of psychoanalysis, which states that the client says everything that comes to mind, as much as possible, and tries not to edit anything out.

Buddha Nature: Buddhism's analogous formulation of a core self.

Childhood Hurts: Psychological harm stemming from early childhood trauma, neglect, maltreatment that often affects how people make choices, use defense mechanisms and form relationships in adulthood.

Compromise Formation: A Freudian concept in which the instincts of aggression and sexuality may come into conflict, resulting in a state of partial gratification of each instinct or wish and partial non-gratification or unfulfillment.

Compulsive Dependency: A component of the Prometheus Chain, where we become exceedingly dependent on others to like us, reflect our values, be interested in us, esteem and love us in order to lessen our self-doubt.

Conscious Emotional Continence: Conscious emotional acceptance of all aspects of ourselves, including that which beforehand was considered unacceptable and unlovable, as the root of happiness.

Containment: A therapeutic outcome in which one gains an increased ability to tolerate his or her feelings, and in doing so gains self-esteem and confidence.

Contempt: Forms as a method of elevating ourselves when we feel badly about ourselves; a feeling that others are worthless, beneath oneself, or deserving of scorn.

Core Self: The expansive foundational self in all human beings that rests in unitive experience of love and primary connectedness with others.

Counterwill: The natural human resistance to being controlled; the initial common "no" to a parent that a two-year-old evidences.

Death Anxiety: A feeling of dread, apprehension or fearfulness when one thinks of the process of dying, or ceasing to exist. Persistent fear of one's own death.

Deficiency Needs: Also known as "d needs." The most fundamental and basic four layers of Maslow's pyramid containing: esteem, friendship and love, security, and physical needs. These needs must be met in order to allow someone to self-actualize.

Depth Psychology: A conceptualization and treatment of the personality based on dynamic and often unconscious motivational elements such as affect, impulses, needs, drive, wishes.

Denial: A primary defense mechanism distinguished by a refusal to acknowledge painful realities, thoughts, feelings or past experiences. A desire to pretend that the painful experiences never happened.

Displaced Needs: When a real need is never gratified, a person can transfer the unmet need into a need to accomplish or obtain a substitute. Often a need for love becomes a displaced need for approval or achievement. Displaced needs never fix the original repressed hurt/need left unmet.

Divine "0": Analogous to Plotinus' Monad, it is an unambivalent, preexistent, unitive experience.

Dual Union: Michael Eigen's term for the simultaneous presence of the two aspects of the self/other experience—the experience of distinction, and the experience of union.

Duality: The state of being in two parts: the way we ultimately see the world and our existential world immersion that is largely unconscious—e.g., good versus evil, right versus wrong, light versus dark etc.

Dying into Process: A surrender to the loss of a part of one's identity through sitting with psychically painful feelings that were previously avoided.

Ego "I": The conscious and knowable part of the self that is in touch with reality and must manage impulses from both the id and the superego.

Ego Instincts: Self-preservative needs and self-love, as opposed to object love; drives that are primarily erotic.

Ego Oriented: The sense of identification with only ourselves, along with a preoccupation with the self at the expense of others.

Ego Logic: Rational judgment, with intuitive or tacit knowledge less evident.

Ego Omnipotence: An inner psychological belief that we should be in charge of all that is around us, which leads us to try to force everything to fit our will, our wants and our needs, including the desire to force others to love us, admire us or put us first. Also known as the need for rulership.

Egocentricity: Holding the idea that one's self (ego) is the center, object and norm of all experience.

Emanations of the Self: The diffusion of the self, meaning the further away from the source, the more distortion of the core self there is (less divine, more negative versions of the self).

Emotional Dwelling: An empathic response in which the listener actively participates in the pain and suffering of the speaker.

Entitlement: When people become fixated or stuck in a childish position of expecting and demanding that the world and others become the good parent they didn't have; an eternal longing and demand that life be made comfortable and easy by others and an anger that arises when this does not occur.

Envy: A feeling of discontent or resentment toward another person due to a desire for the possessions, relationships, or the qualities of another. Envy contains hate in the form of wanting to spoil something for the person who is envied.

Epoche: The mental state in which all judgments about the world are suspended to allow for a fresh look at reality.

Exacting Mechanism: An automatic experience of feeling badly about ourselves when we are against our brothers and sisters in life (occurring both consciously and unconsciously).

False Self: Correlates with the idealized self and is a personality structure developed to conform to the expectations of what others want and expect in the environment. Reads and conforms to the environmental/societal norms deemed to be the most acceptable or perceived as behaving or being in the most glorified way.

Fear of Death: A phenomenon experienced by everyone on the planet, a fear of one's own death or the process of his or her own dying. Associated with death anxiety: the persistent fear or dread of one's own death.

Felt Sense: The inner knowledge or awareness that has not been consciously thought or verbalized. A bodily experience of knowing "something."

Healthy Need: A motivational impulse in the service of emotional growth, self care, affect regulation, and empathic appreciation of the other without which emotional balance and health is impaired. Healthy needs are in the service of love for self and others.

Higher Self: Taoist, Sufi and many modern spiritual/mystical theorists' equivalent to the core self.

Higher Soul: Plotinius' conception of the part of the soul that has some remembrance of the divine; the part of the soul that is involved in trying to reunify the lower soul with the One–divine.

Hubris: Overbearing pride or presumption; arrogance

Human Idiom: According to Christopher Bollas' definition, refers to the unique nucleus of each individual, a figuration of being that is like a kernel that can, under favorable circumstances, evolve and articulate.

Id/"It": A person's internal drives and feelings; contains the instincts including sex, aggression and self-preservation, or the death instinct. The part of the self that is unconscious and outside of awareness.

Id Resistance: A pull in the unconscious to stay attached to our problems. Can be a direct or indirect opposition to change.

Idealized Self: An unrealistically perfectionistic and self-aggrandizing defensive self, although possibly unconscious in nature, that is an attempt to deny vulnerability, shame, anxiety and other dysphoric feelings. Correlates with the concept of false self.

Intentional and Organized Consciousness: A connotation of an organized group of impulses that intentionally seek to defeat emotional growth, love, self-care and the personality.

"K": Wilfred Bion's shorthand expression for knowledge of originary experience.

Kohut's Notion of Self Object: Notion of a primary object that is so present and engaged with the subject that it feels like an extension of one's body.

Liberate: To set free from oppression or suppression.

Libido: The psychic and emotional energy associated with the instinctual biological drives, emanating from the id. Primarily defined as sexual urges and desires.

Life Anxiety: The anxiety of losing oneself in being.

Life Force: The central energy and vitality that moves through all living things. In the unitive state, love is the life force that drives humans.

Loss of Self: Either loss of the self in actuality or loss of the paranoid projection of the ego.

Love Outraged: The idea that all malicious anger and its derivatives—revenge, hate, negative aggression and so forth—are expressions of the need for love being hurt and outraged in earlier development.

Lower Soul: Plotinus' conception of the part of the soul that is separated off and has fallen into vices, character faults and destructive patterns.

Low Self/the Shadow: The aspect of our personality that becomes distorted and misdirected so that love in various ways becomes permutated into hate, avarice, cruelty or envy. Stemming from love outraged.

Magus Object: A phenomenon described by James Grotstein as an internal object or aspect of self-functioning that actually seeks to destroy goodness in the self and the world. A projection of one's own malevolence and ill will, it feels goodness and benevolence in the world is not real. This is analogous to the low self and prevents a person from attaining maturity, growth, love and benevolence because of a lack of trust.

Marriage of Pleasure and Pain: When one takes enjoyment in his or her own pain of self-destructiveness, and self-pity, negative feelings and self-defeating behavior become difficult habits to give up.

Meaninglessness: A sense that the decisions and occurrences of life are devoid of any real significance; purposelessness in life

Monad: The Divine essence of all. The Monad is perfect love and wisdom, and unites everything and everyone.

Moral Masochism: A need for punishment that pushes us toward suffering in other areas of our lives besides our romantic relationships.

Mourning Liberation Process: A process of freeing positive affect that is contained within negative affect or transforming negative affect to positive affect.

Negative Capability: The ability to remain with doubt and uncertainty when self-reflecting and not rush to easy ready-made answers. The capacities of human beings to reject the totalizing constraints of a closed context and explore new understanding of an event or context.

Non-self Centered Subjectivity: A psychological/spiritual phenomenon implicated in a wide range of adaptive behaviors ranging from art to psychoanalytic listening to intimacy. An unconstructed state of being, non-self preoccupied, non-self annulling immersion in whatever one is presently doing, in which there is heightened attentiveness, focus, and clarity.

"O": Originary experience, as noted by Bion, which is a conflation of platonic idealism and Kant's thing-in-itself.

Perfectionism: A compulsive striving for achievement, with standards for oneself that are often unrealistic and contradictory. Perfectionism assumes that if we are just perfect enough we can cancel out our bad feelings, rise above them, and all of our doubts and self-loathing will be assuaged.

Personal Epoch: An important period of distinctive development in an individual's life that has a marked beginning and end and leads to a later, more mature period of development.

Phenomenological Reduction: A systematic attempt to suspend judgments about an event, an experience, or a phenomenon as it appears in consciousness in order to gain a fresh look at reality.

Playing with Aggression: Attempt to enjoy a patient's aggression with him or her in a playful, as-if kind of manner.

Positive Self-assertion: Healthy way of being able to assert oneself in appropriate situations.

Process of Liberation: The process of working through the mask of the false self to the low self. Working through the low self leads to the love outraged of the core self. Working through the layers of the self in this way constitutes a path of transformation. The goal of the liberation process is to liberate the joyful, wise and self-transcendent core self.

Projection: Usually thought of as placing the feelings that we cannot accept in ourselves onto other people. For this text, a projection consists of more: it is actually an unconscious assumption that everyone really feels as we ourselves feel deep down and are unable to accept these feelings.

Prometheus' Chain: Chains that occur throughout life that bind us in Promethean fashion, consisting of six important links: childhood hurt; the anger response to the hurt, or love outraged, which reflects the child's longing for love; low self-esteem and unconscious guilt; gaining relief by bringing on our own punishments; denying negative feelings and destructive attitudes in ourselves and projecting them onto others; and compulsive dependency.

Psyche: The totality of the human mind, including the conscious and unconscious mind.

Psychic Injury: A mental harm, suffering, damage, impairment or dysfunction that interferes with the way in which a person functions. These injuries cause pain that leads to a numbing of our core of love.

Psychic Pain: Anything that is causing psychological pain or discomfort.

Psychological Subjectivity: Each person's own needs, wishes, wants, dreams, ideas and self-direction. The individual idiosyncratic elements to our personalities.

Psycho-spiritual Growth: Transformation of negative traits and faults we find in ourselves to positive life-affirming virtues.

Radical Self-responsibility: A notion that claims that everything we create in our lives is an outpicturing of what is healthy and unhealthy in our personality.

Re-creation/Reenactment of Childhood Hurts: A reconstruction of our childhood difficulties in our later years—e.g., choosing partners who resemble both the positive aspects of our parents as well as the way that they injured us.

Regression: A secondary defense mechanism in which a person reverts to an earlier stage of development in the face of thoughts or impulses that are unacceptable to self-esteem or the ego.

Relational or Intersubjective Technique: These theories place the therapist–client relationship in the forefront of therapeutic change. The therapist's needs, foibles and strengths are taken into consideration along with the client's and are brought into the fray of reenactments of trouble spots within the relationship. Intersubjective therapy focuses on shared meaning and the here-and-now process that occurs between the therapist and the client.

Rigid Ego: When the ego has become too tight or overcontrolled, the ego defends against unconscious negativity with too much repression and other defense mechanisms.

"Rulership" Needs: See Ego Omnipotence

Self-Confrontation: Examining our own behaviors and attitudes to make gainful changes; finding and correcting the flaws in one's own personality and behaviors.

Self-Examination: Examining our own internal thoughts and feelings; reflecting on our own thoughts, feelings, memories and actions to learn from ourself and determine meaning.

Self Object Needs: In infancy children need an immediate felt sense that primary objects are empathically attuned and responsive to their needs.

Self-Reflection: Suspending judgments about how we are supposed to be in an effort to see ourselves as we truly are.

Self-Will: The compulsion to have things go our way at all times regardless of consequences.

Spiritual Bypassing: The phenomenon of leaving behind undeveloped aspects of ourselves, which later come back to haunt us.

Social Feeling: Adler's concept of humans' innate social inclination and the innate human desire to develop bonds or attachments to other human beings.

Spite: A desire to deliberately hurt, annoy or punish someone, which is developed as a way to have the parent or other caregiving authorities bend to the will of the child.

Strong Ego: An ego that is able to contain feelings and examine them for their underlying meaning to eventually transform them back into a more loving state. At this point, the ego has become strong and resilient and is able to accept unflattering desires, wishes, and experiences into awareness. This acceptance allows for mourning and transformation of the unwanted wishes and experiences.

Subjectivity-Embracing Position: When parents understand their child's dysphoria, complaints, feelings and so forth rather than punishing or rejecting the child for them. Helps the child to shape his or her own subjective wishes, wants and desires in alliance with the child's organic readiness to grow and develop.

Sublimation: A defense or process that reorganizes more primitive, conflictual impulses into more benevolent, acceptable ones.

Subpersonalities: Discreet and separated aspects of the personality that function independently of other elements at times.

Surrender by Emanuel Ghent: Often accompanied by dread and death, and/or clarity, relief, even ecstasy; the decision to discover and the process of discovering one's identity, sense of self, sense of wholeness and sense of unity with other living beings.

"T": Wilfred Bion's shorthand expression of Transformation of Originary experience.

Transcendent Function: A higher order integrative function in the personality that tends toward integration and resolution of conflictual elements.

Transference: The unconscious phenomenon of displacing and transferring feelings from one person to another in therapy. Feelings from previous and current relationships existing outside of the session are often transferred onto the therapist.

Transforming Duality Process: A process that points at our deepest psychological fears and anxieties and aims at their transformation; a process of containing and accepting negative feelings in order to move beyond existential fear.

Trauma: Especially potent in early life, a severe emotional or physical experience that causes damage: lasting physical, psychological, and/or emotional impairment.

Unconscious Guilt: An ego state resulting from a conflict between the "should have done" aims of the superego and the ego. An automatic sense of feeling badly about oneself and undeserving of good things, leading to an unconscious, bitter resentment.

Unhealthy Needs: Needs that are against love and therefore against the real self and others. Motivational impulses that are against or intend to do harm to our real self and others and are based on issues of vanity, the appearance of power and egoism.

Unitive Consciousness: An experience of "oneness" in whatever degree—e.g., oneness with the self, with others, with humanity etc.

Unitive State of the World: The ultimate reality and truth that illuminates the awareness of the interconnectedness with others and all life. Brings about a felt sense of empathy with others and a connectedness to our feelings that can resolve ethical dilemmas where outer rules fail us.

Weak Ego: When the ego is too weak, feelings threaten to override the control and balance in the personality. The weak ego contains real feelings that have deviated from their origin in love, and have become negative and destructive due to trauma or the pains of life and our own ignorance.

Will: The impulse to self-direct, to affect our world and create ourselves.

Index

Other Books by University Professors Press

www.universityprofessorspress.com

The Polarized Mind: Why It's Killing Us and What We Can Do About It
By Kirk Schneider

Bare: Psychotherapy Stripped
By Jacqueline Simon Gunn & Carlo DeCarlo

Humanistic Contributions for Psychology 101: Growth, Choice, and Responsibility
By Richard Bargdill & Rodger Broomé

An Artist's Thought Book: Intriguing Thoughts About the Artistic Process
By Richard Bargdill

The Buddha, the Bike, the Couch, and the Circle: A Festschrift for Dr. Robert Unger
By Michael M. Dow, Francis J. Kaklauskas, & Elizabeth Olson

Stay Awhile: Poetic Narratives on Multiculturalism and Diversity
By Louis Hoffman & Nathaniel Granger, Jr.

Capturing Shadows: Poetic Encounters Along the Path of Grief & Loss
By Louis Hoffman & Michael Moats

About the Author

Franklin Sollars, PhD is a licensed psychologist, author, and screenwriter. He is a certified psychoanalyst who identifies with the emerging cadre of psychoanalytic thinkers described as Psychoanalytic Mystics. Founding president of the Michigan Society for Integrative Psychoanalytic Studies, he is currently its vice president for programs. Dr Sollars is a professor at the Michigan School of Professional Psychology and the clinical director of Sollars and Associates Integrative Psychological Services.

CPSIA information can be obtained
at www.ICGtesting.com
Printed in the USA
FSOW03n0917120516
20269FS